GLENWOOD CANYON

From Origin to Interstate

GLENWOOD CANYON

From Origin to Interstate

CONRAD F. SCHADER

REGIO
ALTA
PUBLICATIONS
GOLDEN,CO 80403

ISBN: 0-9634479-1-2

Subject Outline:
    History, Colorado, Garfield County
       Glenwood Canyon
           rivers
           railroads
           highways
           Native Americans
           settlements
           mines & mining
           national forests
           environment
           outdoor recreation

Design and typography by Shadow Canyon Graphics, Evergreen, Colorado.

Front Cover: Looking downriver below Shoshone Dam, August 1985. Conrad F. Schader photo.

Printed in the United States of America
First Edition

To

LBS

and

FCS

and all the others who have

traveled the canyon's

trails, roads, and rails

CONTENTS

PREFACE

During a drive from Denver to Salt Lake City around 1950, we became acquainted with Glenwood Canyon and stayed overnight near the river in Glenwood Springs. According to fading recollections of the trip, Radio Station KGLN was nearby, and owner Jerry Fitch, though he himself was the station operator that evening, took time to explain the operation to this novice radio announcer and offer insights concerning the business.

That trip was the precursor of many pleasant days in the canyon area. The visits became more frequent in the early 1970s, when the planned route of Interstate 70 through the canyon was a subject of widespread controversy and emotional debate, and an attempt began then to capture the entire canyon on film before the start of construction.

In the mid 1970s, research began concerning the canyon's history, and a book began to take shape. The final phase of the work involved more photography, acquisition of archival materials, and recording of first-person recollections.

Because a complete history of Glenwood Springs would itself fill at least one sizeable volume, it was necessary to set parameters to bring the city's long and varied past within practical dimensions. It was decided to concentrate on the city's origins, its most famous events and attractions, and some of the factors that have steered its economy.

Completion of the book was possible only with the cooperation of many people and organizations, and their contributions are gratefully acknowledged.

Bill and Elva Dennison of Denver provided information that led to a veritable network of people who had been associated with the canyon in various ways, making possible the gathering of first-person accounts. The staff of Frontier Historical Museum in Glenwood Springs, especially Sue Plush and Willa Soncarty, located articles and photos that were essential to this book.

Loretta B. and Frank C. Schader, my late parents, helped photograph the canyon and track the multi-faceted controversy surrounding the route of I-70.

Special thanks to Dan Hopkins, Pauline C. Haberman, and Carl Sorrentino of Colorado Department of Transportation; Denver Public Library Western History Department, especially A. D. Mastrogiuseppe; Colorado Historical Society library, Denver, especially Rebecca Lintz; Jefferson County Library System, especially the Golden branch; L. J. Savage Library, Western State College of Colorado, Gunnison; U.S. Geological Survey Library, Denver Federal Center; Bureau of Land Management Colorado Office, Lakewood; U.S. Archives and Records Administration, Washington and Denver, particularly Joan Howard, Denver; the office of the Colorado Secretary of State; Terry Wilson for permission to use an especially valuable Vista-Dome Monument photo from the Schutte Collection at Glenwood Springs; and Ray L. Dudley for technical assistance concerning the story of Shoshone Hydroelectric Plant.

A number of other people provided photographs and information and granted interviews that were important to completion of the canyon story. Their contributions are evident in the text, photo credits, and bibliography.

It is hoped that the account herein constitutes an accurate and interesting history of the splendid canyon and its settlements.

M.R. Campbell photo U.S. Geological Survey 1137

Even-belted quartzite in Glenwood Canyon wall. Looking east along
Rio Grande track, 1915.

I

ROCK AND RIVER

Roots of Glenwood Canyon in northwestern Colorado lie deep. They reach into an obscure eon prior to the building of the Rocky Mountains.

The very fact of this 12.5-mile canyon's excavation has left many of these roots, layers of rock deposited through the ages, accessible to geologists who probe the characteristics of the pre-historic earth. While definition of the rock layers here began in the 1800s, subsequent research added, and continues to add, insights to the powerful, earth-altering events that contributed to the canyon's formation.

From the one-time settlement of Siloam Springs on the east to the world-famous spa of Glenwood Springs on the west, the many rock layers in the cliffs are apparent even to travelers who drive Interstate 70 without pause. Closer views of the strata are facilitated by rest areas along the highway, a canyon-long recreation path, and a number of trails through the side canyons.

First known by English-speaking people as the Grand River Canyon, the gorge held that name until the Garfield County Commission passed a resolution in 1914 favoring a change.

About 0.4 mile of the canyon lies in Eagle County, while the major portion stretches westward through Garfield County.

ROCK OLDER THAN THE HILLS

Uplifting of the White River Plateau, faulting, erosion, and downcutting by the Colorado River all are responsible for the formation of Glenwood Canyon. From a point near Shoshone Dam, the rock formations arch downward toward both ends of the canyon. As a result, rock formations seen at river level progress from younger to older and then from older to younger as a person travels the length of the canyon. Because of faulting, older rocks also appear in similar but shorter progressions near both ends of the canyon.

The oldest exposed rock is at least 570 million years of age. Tremendous heat and pressure formed it from pre-existing sediments long before the building of today's Rocky Mountains. This dark-gray granite originated in the Proterozoic Era of geologic time. During that era, mountains formed, but erosion picked away at them for millions of years, until the landscape became nearly level, and the ancient rivers barely flowed. Hard, crystalline rock that once lay at the core of an ancient mountain range is especially evident near Shoshone Dam and the power plant a couple of miles downstream. Pink and white veins in this rock are feldspar and quartz.

Region Was Under Influence of Sea

Layers above the granite are sedimentary rocks that originated as deposits left by a shifting, inland sea. The sea advanced and receded across the Glenwood area a number of times during that Paleozoic Era, leaving layers of sand, mud, small stones, and shells and other remains of early marine forms of life over a period of more than 250 million years. Heat, pressure, and chemical action transformed the sediments to stone — sandstone, shale, limestone, and dolomite. These strata dominate the walls of the canyon.

The oldest of the Paleozoic formations is a product of the Cambrian Period. This metamorphosed formation once was a bed of sand. The constituent quartz (silica dioxide) cemented it into sandstone. Heat and pressure later changed the sandstone to quartzite, a much tougher rock. The 500-foot-thick bed is called the Sawatch Formation. It takes its name from the Sawatch Range, one of Colorado's principal mountain ranges, where the formation is readily observed. The north end of the range is not far east of Glenwood Canyon. At the range's south end, beginning at Poncha Springs, lies the San Luis Valley. Sawatch is a Ute expression meaning "waters of the blue earth," and it is believed that the expression originated when the valley was the floor of a large lake.*

In Glenwood Canyon, the boundary between gray Precambrian granite and brown Sawatch cliffs is obvious because of the color difference and an angular unconformity where the two formations meet. Rather than being parallel, they meet at an angle. An unconformity indicates a period of time that is not represented by evidence of events that took place then.

All of the canyon's formations above the Sawatch are also from the Paleozoic Era. The youngest rock is from the beginnings of the Pennsylvanian Period, evidenced by remnants of the Belden Formation. Time since the early part of the Pennsylvanian Period is not represented by surviving deposits. It is believed that later depositions took place but were destroyed by erosion, a conclusion based on the presence of such younger deposits to the east and west in the subsurface.

It is interesting to note that the White River Plateau is at least as old as the Manitou Formation. Geologists say the area was then under water, but in location and topography the plateau closely resembled the structure of today.

---

* *Sawatch* and the original *Saguache* stem from efforts to present a spoken expression in written form. The Utes had no written language.

GLENWOOD CANYON, GENERAL REPRESENTATION OF EXPOSED ROCK FORMATIONS

Era	Period	Formation	Approx. Thickness (feet)	Remarks	Age (millions of years)
	Pennsylvanian	Belden	—	Poorly represented. Gray shale. Major uplift early in period.	325
	unconformity				
	Mississippian	Leadville	200	Cliffs of dolomite & variety of limestone types, gray to brownish gray. Band of red shale at upper end.	365
	unconformity; inconspicuous				
	Devonian	Chaffee Group Dyer Formation Parting Formation	250	Dolomite, limestone, quartzose sandstone. Many gray to greenish-gray ledges. Some red shale. Fossil evidence of marine life — brachiopods, bryozoans, fish, mollusks, corals, algae.	410
	unconformity; erosion probably destroyed Silurian Period strata				
	Ordovician	Manitou Tie Gulch Member Dead Horse Member	150	Cliffs: dolomite & limestone, brown hue. Much flat-pebble conglomerate. White River Plateau resembled today's plateau in location & topography, but was under water much of time.	440 510
		Dotsero Clinetop Member Glenwood Canyon Member	100	Mostly flat-pebble dolomite or limestone conglomerate. Upper 5 to 10 ft., Clinetop Member, is stromatolite carbonate, white with lavender hue.	510
	Cambrian	Sawatch	500	Mostly quartzose sandstones, brown beds. Formation meets underlying Precambrian at angle.	520
	unconformity				
	Precambrian	—	—	Lightly represented. Crystalline rock, dark gray with pink & white intrusions. Mountains built during era were worn down by erosion. Sea began to move into Colorado from west at end of era.	570 2500

Oldest rock in canyon — from Precambrian Period — originated in Proterozoic Era. All surviving depositions younger than Proterozoic took place during Paleozoic Era.

Principal source: Campbell, "Lower Paleozoic Systems, White River Plateau"; Conrad F. Schader table

According to scientists, the earth's crust consists of a number of rigid plates. Expanding sea floors pressed the North American Plate slowly westward over a Pacific plate, and the resulting stresses warped, folded, broke, and otherwise deformed the crust along a weak stretch in the North American Plate. This action beginning about 300 million years ago created mountains known as the Ancestral Rockies.

Another period of such mountain building about 60 million years ago formed the superstructure of today's Rocky Mountains. The White River Plateau and other structures rose. With the North American Plate being pressed westward more than 1,000 miles, continued stresses in the crust eventually pushed all of Colorado some 5,000 feet higher, to the present elevation.

The weight of uplifted rock and shifting seas, erosion, and volcanic activity at previous ruptures in the crust subsequently shaped the Rockies into a form roughly akin to that which we observe today. The grinding action of glaciers, deposition of glacial debris, and continuing erosion later altered the landscape and produced the present topography.

RIVER TAKES NEW COURSE, CARVES CANYON

Geologists believe that the original course of the Colorado River was more northerly than it is now. It flowed approximately from Middle Park westward across the present beginnings of the Yampa River and into the headwaters of today's White River.

Much of our knowledge of Glenwood Canyon's formation evolved from the pioneering work begun by John Wesley Powell in the second half of the 1860s. Powell, father of the U.S. Geological Survey and the science of physical geology, competed with such contemporaries as F. V. Hayden and Clarence King in studies of the geology, geography, topography, and ethnology of Colorado. Today's quadrangle system of topographic mapping originated with Powell.

More than 10 million years ago, the Colorado found its present course near the south end of the White River Plateau and began to carve Glenwood Canyon. It was an irregular course governed by the youngest, surface rocks. While the uplift of the plateau continued, the river succeeded in maintaining its course by cutting through the obstruction, much as it did far downstream in the Grand Canyon of Arizona. In more precise terms, according to a U.S. Geological Survey publication, the river probably was superimposed on the White River uplift; erosion obliterated the top layers through which it cut originally. However, deepening of the gorge was evidently a result of subsequent downcutting during continuation of the uplift. This means that Glenwood Canyon "is in part antecedent." It existed to some depth prior to the final 2,000 feet of plateau uplift. One sixth of the plateau uplift "seems to have occurred" during the past 12 million years "as if deformation there has progressed linearly with time," according to the Geological Survey.

Canyon carving within the past 20 millenia gained the strength of runoff from melting glaciers that extended from the highest mountains down to the 9,000-foot elevation. Laden with debris, these huge flows of fast-moving water gave the river additional abrasive power to cut into its rock bed. After chewing downward in places through all of the Paleozoic layers, the Colorado eventually followed vertical cracks to bite into the hard and very old Proterozoic rock below.

The result was a canyon some 2,000 feet deep in places. From east to west, the level of the river sloped downward 370 feet, dropping to an elevation of 5,750 feet at the canyon mouth in present Glenwood Springs. That gave the river an average rate of descent of 29.6 feet per mile for its run through the canyon.

Canyon Deepening Now Very Slow

River flow lessened, and its erosive capability decreased after the Ice Age glaciers melted. While the Colorado continues today to deepen the canyon, the rate of downcutting is slow.

Conrad F. Schader

Some sedimentary layers deposited early in Paleozoic Era.
North wall of canyon beside U.S. 6 & 24, October 1976.

Water storage and diversion projects in the headwaters area reduce the river volume. In addition, the pool of water extending upstream from Shoshone Dam slows the currents in the upper part of the canyon, causes a reduction of downcutting, and actually promotes some buildup of the river bed as heavier matter settles out of the slowing currents.

Erosion of the bed is especially slow between Shoshone Dam and the Shoshone Power Plant. This 2.5-mile stretch carries a flow only when river volume exceeds the 1905 water rights being exercised by the plant. These are the oldest major rights on the Western Slope of Colorado, and they work to the Colorado River's benefit by helping to insure a continued flow from its source all the way down to the dam. Water users along this lengthy stretch must allow enough water to pass downstream to meet the senior rights of the power plant.

Low river volume due to light snowpack and hot, dry weather in 1994 spurred plant operators to issue an early call, a demand for the plant's share of water, at the end of June. To meet this demand, upstream water users with lesser rights were obligated to divert water into the Colorado to provide the power plant's guaranteed amount. To satisfy the requirement, users with lower priorities channeled water into the Colorado from a storage reservoir containing supplies for customers east of the mountains. The 1994 call was the earliest such demand on the Colorado's flow since 1977. In 1993, when river flow was much higher, Shoshone issued no call until September.

Shoshone's seniority also benefits the river system downstream, because the diverted water runs back into the river after powering the plant's generators. Word of a Denver offer to purchase the water rights held by the Shoshone plant surfaced in 1991. The possibility of such a sale angered Western Slope interests who have been increasingly concerned regarding attempts to divert additional water to the thirsty cities east of the Continental Divide. In the 1980s, the Denver water system drew 70 percent of its supply from the Colorado River Basin. The *Rocky Mountain News* quoted a water attorney's comment that such a purchase would " 'change the whole hydrology of the river system.' " However, under a 20-year agreement reached in 1986, Denver already had the right to divert the water and pay the power company for any resulting loss of generating capacity.

The Colorado River headwaters lie on the slopes of the Continental Divide in Rocky Mountain National Park. Prior to its entry into Glenwood Canyon, the river receives waters of the Eagle River and numerous other tributary streams.

Peak flow on the Colorado generally occurs during spring, when runoff from rains and melting snows is greatest, although weather conditions occasionally delay the peak into July. After unusually heavy buildups of mountain snow followed by suddenly warmer weather, river flows can exceed 22,000 cubic feet per second (165,000 gallons per second), as was the case in May 1984. Lowest flows occur generally from autumn through winter, when ice and snow lock up much of the tributary runoff.

Water temperatures in the canyon cover a range of some 30 degrees Fahrenheit and depend on location and season. Winter readings are predominantly just above freezing, while summer measurements reach the mid 60s.

River By Any Other Name Still The Colorado

Before it became the Colorado, the river that pours through Glenwood Canyon had a number of other names. It appeared on various maps as the Blue, Bunkara, Nahunkahrea, North Fork of the Grand, and Grand. Spanish Governor Juan de Oñate named it Rio Grande de Buena Esperanza in the 1600s. Franciscan priest Silvestre Velez de Escalante, who crossed the river in the mid 1700s near DeBeque, downstream from Glenwood Springs, called it Rio de San Rafael.

The name Grand, which originated with French trappers, became dominant and remained in use 45 years after Colorado's 1876 achievement of statehood. Meantime, the lengthy stretch of river downstream of the Grand's junction with the Green River in Utah bore the name Colorado.

When a river had two tributaries, it was the custom to give the larger tributary the same name as the mainstem river. In this case, the Colorado had two tributaries, the Grand and the Green, with the Green being the larger.

State Senator Edward T. Taylor early in the 20th century championed a bill to change the name of the Grand to Colorado, but the measure failed. Taylor soon became a member of the U.S. House of Representatives, and there was no definitive action on the name until 1921. State Senator Ollie Bannister gained passage of the old Taylor bill, and Governor Oliver H. Shoup signed it on March 24. In the same year, a congressional resolution, effective July 25, echoed the state legislation. An 80-mile section in eastern Utah still carried the name Grand but later came into conformity through Utah legislative action.

A number of names in Colorado remain as testimony to the river's influence under the name Grand. They include Grand Lake, Grand County, the Grand Valley, and Grand Junction.

Traveling the River

While John Wesley Powell's survey parties studied Glenwood Canyon, Powell's famous float expeditions of the 1860s began far to the west, on the Green River above its junction with the Colorado.

As part of a long expedition on and along the Colorado, Harold Leich passed through Glenwood Canyon in 1933. He floated the river where possible and portaged his wooden kayak around the worst rapids.

Later, at least one attempt to navigate an unrunnable section ended in disaster. Using a 26-foot rubber raft, a party of Aspen men attempted the fearsome rapids just below Shoshone Dam in May 1956. Scores of motorists stopped beside U.S. Highway 6 and 24 to watch the three floaters board the life raft and enter the raging river and its waves as high as 30 feet.

Citing reports from witnesses, the *Glenwood Post* said the 20-man raft successfully negotiated a large wave and floated

Colorado Historical Society 25144

Portion of Shoshone Rapids, a.k.a. Cottonwood Falls, at relatively low river level. Date unknown.

into an eddy where it paused briefly before being captured again by the river current. The churning water turned the raft somewhat sideways as it swept the craft into a huge wave that overturned the raft and threw it onto a crest.

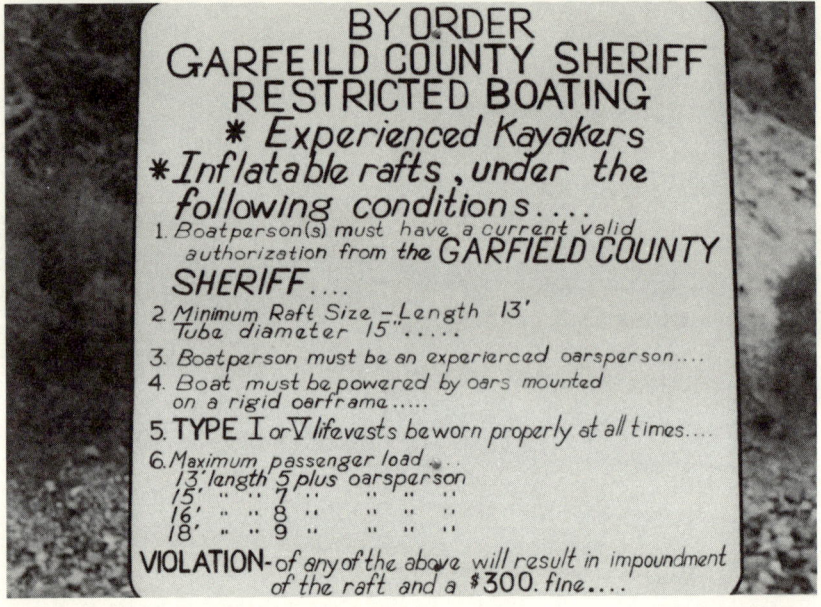

BY ORDER
GARFEILD COUNTY SHERIFF
RESTRICTED BOATING
* Experienced Kayakers
*Inflatable rafts, under the
following conditions....
1. Boatperson(s) must have a current valid
   authorization from the GARFIELD COUNTY
   SHERIFF....
2. Minimum Raft Size - Length 13'
   Tube diameter 15".....
3. Boatperson must be an experienced oarsperson....
4. Boat must be powered by oars mounted
   on a rigid oarframe.....
5. TYPE I or V lifevests be worn properly at all times....
6. Maximum passenger load ....
   13' length 5 plus oarsperson
   15'   "   " 7   "   "   "   "   "
   16'   "   " 8   "   "   "   "   "
   18'   "   " 9   "   "   "   "   "
VIOLATION- of any of the above will result in impoundment
   of the raft and a $300. fine....

Conrad F. Schader

Sign beside Colorado River, Glenwood Canyon, June 1977.

Twenty-six-year-old Robert Mann was presumed drowned. Witnesses said he appeared to be unconscious when they spotted him momentarily after the accident. His two companions managed to reach the river bank, 36-year-old Kenneth Moore with a dislocated shoulder and 26-year-old John Zerfluh with no injuries.

Today, it remains impossible to float the river's entire course through the canyon. Shoshone Dam and other hazards pose the threat of ambush for floaters who fail to get off the water soon enough. And the stretch from the Shoshone Dam down to the power plant often carries no flow. One look at the huge jumble of rocks and steep drops offers convincing evidence that the "unrunnable" designation is appropriate there, even when there is sufficient water.

With due caution, appropriate equipment, and experience to match the class of water involved, floaters can safely travel parts of the canyon. Some runs are suitable for novices and open canoes. Others require expert floaters with equipment appropriate for heavy water. Classifications of the runnable sections change with variations in river level. According to Doug Wheat in *The Floaters Guide to Colorado*, some of the "biggest water in the state" lies between the power plant and Grizzly Creek. There are rapids with such foreboding names as Upper and Lower Superstition, Man Eater, Tombstone, and The Wall.

A number of companies guide floaters on the river and also offer trips in company boats. Booking a trip on a craft operated by one of these licensed outfitters is a way to gain some familiarity with the river while professionals do the work. Colorado requires the use of life vests.

CAVES FORMED

Colorado's greatest concentration of known caves lies in the White River Plateau area. Natural forces, mainly chemical action supported by ground water, gradually carved numerous caves in the Leadville Limestone Formation within the past two-million years. An estimated 90 percent of them remain undiscovered, because they have no openings to the surface.

Vapor Caves Open To All

Best known of the caverns in and near the canyon are the Vapor Caves near the big pool in the northeast corner of Glenwood Springs. At the time of this writing, they are the only commercially operated caverns in the area. Hundreds, if not thousands, of years before Colorado appeared on any map, inhabitants of the region sought the vapors and heat of the caves and nearby mudholes in efforts to alleviate a variety of ailments. After the lands came into the hands of participants in the westward migration, commercial development attracted tourists and fame to the Vapor Caves.

Development in the first half of the 1890s, by the same people who built the big pool and Hotel Colorado, included enlargement of the caves and construction of a wooden enclosure at the entrances.

In these four grottos, hot gases percolate from the depths and raise the air temperature to 112 degrees Fahrenheit. Composition of the gases is largely carbon dioxide laced with vapors of sulphur and other minerals. The gases are accompanied by a five-gallon-per-minute flow of 122-degree water.

Some Other Caves Outlined

More than two dozen other, known caves are in the Glenwood Canyon locale. They are visited by scientists and by hobbyists called *spelunkers* or *cavers*. Cavers sometimes allow other interested persons to accompany them.

Before highlighting a few of these other caves, a warning is necessary concerning them. Exploration can be hazardous to both the explorer and the cave environment. It requires proper equipment and procedures. People who are "not prepared for the caving experience can really get into trouble," according to Bill Kight, Heritage Resource Manager for the White River National Forest. Caves are not only an important resource, but they are also fragile and irreplaceable. "You want the public to know about the resources, but you also want them to take care of them and know what they're getting into," said Kight in a 1995 interview.

A number of the caves are on private property, but most are on U.S. Government land managed by the Forest Service. A number of cave entrances have gates to block unauthorized entry. It is against the law to break protective gates and to damage or remove formations and artifacts from caves. Persons interested in exploration should contact the U.S. Forest Service in Glenwood Springs for information on visitation possibilities well in advance of any contemplated trip.

Hubbard's and Hobo

With at least 3,000 feet of passageways, Hubbard's is the eleventh longest in the state. Among the Glenwood area's best known, its entrance is visible high in the south wall of the canyon, across the river from Shoshone Power Plant. The name probably comes from Henry Hubbard. He and Griffith B. Jones discovered the cave and viewed its cave coral and other formations while prospecting for minerals in the 19th century.

Hobo served as a one-room stopover for transients at the east edge of Glenwood Springs. Smoke, ash, and heavy use virtually destroyed this cavern's formations many years ago.

Fairy Cave and Pete's Pit

Privately owned Fairy Cave in Iron Mountain is the best-known cavern in the Glenwood Canyon locale. Ranking among Colorado's largest, it is the fifth longest, with a surveyed length of 7,800 feet. The vertical relief is 200 feet, giving it a tie for seventh place in that category.

The Charles Darrow family operated the cave commercially for a time, and the network of passageways and at least six chambers underwent considerable development, including electric lighting. At the time of an 1897 article in *The Avalanche* of Glenwood Springs, the largest chamber measured 12 by 200 feet. Work was underway on a 125-foot tunnel from the cave to an exterior balcony high above the river. The observation balcony perched on a cliff with a "wall of rock 100 feet high, above, and an almost perpendicular abyss, down, down, 1,200 feet below." The article described varied and "fantastic" formations within the cave and reported "hundreds of stalactites, stalagmites and pillars." Around 1900, the cave was a popular destination for tourists traveling to the site on foot, on burros, and in horse-drawn carriages.

Operations ended around 1917. In the 1960s, cave enthusiasts bought the property for preservation purposes.

In the same area is Pete's Pit. The three chambers are reportedly in vertical sequence, an uncommon occurrence in Colorado.

Cave of the Chimes, Cave of the Clouds, Defiance Cavern

On private property in the same general area is Cave of the Chimes. It is about 250 feet long.

Surveyors found Cave of the Clouds, originally known as Alexander's Cave, in the canyon's north side during the 1880s. This two-room cave near the west end of the canyon once exhibited some of the state's most impressive formations.

Work in the Grandview Mine near Fort Defiance purportedly revealed a natural room called Defiance Cavern. The mine closed after an explosion.

II

THE UTES AND
THEIR ANCESTORS

Some scientists believe that American Indians originated in Asia and traveled to North America no later than 10,000 B.C. via a bridge of land that now lies beneath waters of the Bering Strait. But tribal traditions say that ancestors of today's Utes lived in the West since the dawn of human life here.

There is increasing evidence that Colorado was home to a sizeable population of hunter-gatherers, called Paleo Indians, during the Stone Age. And results of recent studies support the idea of an ancestral Ute presence in the Glenwood Canyon region thousands of years before the arrival of Europeans.

IMPORTANT DISCOVERIES NOTED

Two discoveries in recent years broadened our knowledge of early human activities in northwestern Colorado. While neither occurred in Glenwood Canyon, both provided intriguing evidence of humans who probably had an acquaintance with the canyon near the end of the last Ice Age. It was a difficult existence. Survival required much physical effort, persistence, and ingenuity. These people depended on wild animals as sources of food as well as materials for shelter, clothing, and some tools. Some of the animals of that time were much larger and perhaps fiercer than today's game animals. Among them were giant bison and ground sloths.

Around 1990, members of a group exploring the narrow, muddy passageways of a White River National Forest cave found the scattered bones of a human skeleton. Officials secured the cave against unauthorized entry, and researchers from the Federal Government and Washington University of St. Louis launched studies of the cave and the skeletal remains.

Some results of the studies emerged publicly in 1993. The skeleton was that of a man who died of undetermined cause 8,000 years ago. Elevation of the discovery site was around 10,000 feet. Never before in North America had a human skeleton of that age been found at such a high elevation.

The man stood five feet, five inches tall, did considerable walking on steep terrain, and died at the approximate age of 40. DNA tests indicated a relationship between this man and some Native American tribes.

The condition of this Ute ancestor's teeth evidenced a nomadic way of life rather than that of a village dweller, according to Kenny Frost, a Ute who works as a consultant to Federal agencies concerning Ute subjects, especially archaeological matters. Frost said the condition of the teeth indicated a diet based largely on meat, rather than on tooth-eroding grains. "He also had a slight arthritic condition in his back, which indicated that he carried things on his back," said Frost. The man apparently used a torch to light his way, a conclusion reached after analysis of charcoal fragments and smudges at the discovery site. Because of the characteristics of the cavern, it probably was not used as a home. Some DNA studies and investigations into the geomorphology and geology of the cave continued in 1995.

In accordance with Federal law, the nearest tribe, the Southern Ute, was consulted. The ancient man's remains were given to the Utes for burial conforming to Ute traditions.

Researchers from the University of Colorado in 1993 revisited the site of a prehistoric mine that was first studied in 1985. They found that this mine complex at Rabbit Ears Pass, not far from Steamboat Springs, was larger than previously thought. In this massive network of trenches and 200 pits, ancestors of the Utes pried out five feet of sandstone to expose hard, underlying quartzite veins. They mined the quartzite and fashioned it into projectile points, knives, awls, and other tools for hunting, skinning, and sewing.

Because of the size of the mined area, investigators mentioned a probability that the miners conducted large-scale trade in quartzite and quartzite tools with other tribes of the West. According to newspaper accounts, some projectile points from the area matched a style used in 6,000 B.C. Others matched those used by the Utes no earlier than the 15th century A.D.

MIGRATION BELIEVED CONTINUOUS

Lewis H. Morgan wrote of continuous migration from north to south along the mountain ranges. Traditions of some Indians living in Mexico "at the time of Spanish discovery" spoke of ancestral migration from the north.

Ancestors of the Utes found their way into present Colorado from the west and north as many as 9,000 years ago, according to James Jefferson in *The Southern Utes*. Around 2,000 years ago, people who spoke the Shoshonean language distanced themselves from a number of groups that shared their Uto-Aztecan heritage. These early Utes became well established in what is now Colorado. They ranged over all of Colorado and hunted in southern Wyoming, eastern Utah, northern Arizona, Kansas, Nebraska, New Mexico as far south as Santa Fe, the western half of Texas, and up into the Dakotas. "That was the territorial range of the Utes," said Kenny Frost, who described himself as a go-between to facilitate the exchange of viewpoints and contribute to better understanding between the Colorado Utes and government agencies. "The

Glenwood area was pretty much the heart of Ute country," he said.

United States explorers penetrated the frontier in the early 1800s to investigate lands acquired from other countries. Immigrants of European descent soon sought their fortunes here, bringing with them the desire to own, control, and change the land. Land ownership was a foreign concept to the Utes. They believed that the land was the property, perhaps the embodiment, of a Supreme Being and that it belonged to all humans as caretakers. It is understandable that the Native Americans felt fear and moral outrage when miners blasted the rock, settlers erected fences, and hunters decimated herds of buffalo for the hides or merely for sport.

Encouraged by government policies, America's westward migration soon resulted in the separation of Colorado's Ute population into seven loosely confederated bands. Each band had its own chief and council, largely because the United States needed spokesmen with whom to negotiate Ute concessions. There was no person who could speak for all of the Utes, and the United States eventually appointed Chief Ouray to serve in that capacity.

Having previously acquired horses from the Spanish, the Utes had become expert horsemen. Food procurement — hunting game and gathering wild grains, roots, nuts, and berries — monopolized the time of the nomadic Utes.

In the warmer months, the search for food required families to scatter widely across the higher elevations. In winter, families sought the lower elevations and camped together.

After the Utes had been prompted into formation of bands, the White River band was the one most closely associated with the Glenwood Canyon area. Members of that band roamed a large area extending from the Colorado River northward and westward across the White River Plateau to the northwestern corner of present Colorado. These people wintered along the Colorado, White, or Green rivers. They, and others, often visited hot springs at both ends of Glenwood Canyon and the vapor caves at the west end in efforts to cleanse their wounds, cure disease, and alleviate body aches.

Colorado Historical Society 1012

Top row: Chief Washington, Ouray's sister Susan, Johnston No. 2 (married to Susan), Capt. Jack, John. Middle row: Uriah M. Curtis, Agent J. B. Thompson of Ute Agency at Denver, Agent Charles Adams of Ute Agency south of Gunnison, U.S. negotiator Otto Mears. Bottom row: Tabeguache sub-chief Guero, Ouray's second wife Chipeta, Chief Ouray, Tabeguache Chief Piah. Photo circa 1874, when Ouray was about 41, Chipeta 10 years younger.

MINING SPAWNS RESTRICTIONS ON UTES

News of gold discoveries in 1858 at present Denver, and the following year near the sites of Idaho Springs and Central City, lured thousands of hopeful people to what is now Colorado. Prospectors fanned out across the mountains and made additional discoveries. Farmers, ranchers, merchants, and opportunists of every description joined the rush to the Rockies.

In January 1860, Glenwood Canyon was a part of Utah Territory. The closest post office was a newly established operation in Breckinridge, according to Bauer and others in *Colorado Postal History*.* Colorado achieved territorial status in February 1861 and statehood on August 1, 1876, drawing additional attention to the region and attracting more immigrants.

Utes Lose Ground

Many immigrants saw the Indian presence as a threat to their families and a hindrance to their businesses. The United States and the Utes executed a number of treaties, and with each successive treaty the Utes gave up more of their range and freedom. As miners and settlers spotted new areas of opportunity, they looked to the Federal Government to open more lands for development. This pressure on the nation's lawmakers and executives drew strength from rumors, most of them false, of Ute attacks on miners and settlers.

In 1868 all seven Ute bands agreed to a new treaty restricting them to a reservation encompassing most of Colorado Territory's Western Slope, all the lands west of 107 degrees west longitude. This revised eastern boundary passed very close to the eastern end of Glenwood Canyon, so the canyon remained within the reservation.

Provocations Breed Tragedy at White River

Tensions reached a critical point in 1879 around the White River Indian Agency near the present town of Meeker. The resulting violence acted as a catalyst, forcing the Utes to relinquish most of their remaining land in Colorado.

The United States had a treaty obligation to provide the Utes with supplies and money but failed to deliver them to the agency on a timely basis. Meantime, the Utes grew increasingly

---

*   The spelling was changed later to Breckenridge.

resentful of efforts by Agent Nathan C. Meeker to force them to abandon their hunting-gathering traditions and become farmers.

While apparently well intentioned, Meeker's tactics were misguided and heavy handed. The agent seriously offended and provoked the Indians when he plowed an irrigation ditch through a pasture or exercise area the Utes used for the horses they valued so highly.

Signs of resentment, including a confrontation during which a Ute leader shoved him against a wall, led Meeker to fear for his life, and he requested military assistance. When an advance detachment of 160 Fort Rawlins cavalry, led by Major T. T. Thornburgh, neared the agency in September, Ute leader Captain Jack and some 300 cohorts trapped them in Red Canyon. The ambush came despite earlier assurances of safe passage from a Ute delegation that approached Thornburgh along his route.

Major Thornburgh died during the initial attack. Sporadic fighting lasted almost a week, nearly annihilating the army contingent. The Utes abandoned the siege when the full Fort Rawlins force finally arrived.

Shortly after the canyon ambush, Chief Douglas led about two dozen Utes in an attack on the agency itself, killing Agent Meeker and eleven other men. The attackers took women and children as hostages but released them later.

United States Presses Ute Relocation

The violence at the White River Agency ignited public outrage, intensified fears among settlers, and aided opponents of the Ute presence in Colorado. A Ute delegation, invited to Washington for negotiations in early 1880, signed an agreement requiring the Utes to move onto specified reservations in southwestern Colorado, western Colorado near present Grand Junction, northwestern New Mexico, and Utah. Congress approved the agreement, and by December the required 75 percent of male, adult Utes signed the pact.

Implementation of the agreement began almost immediately but deviated from the original intent of a key provision. By a liberal interpretation of the agreement, the United States eliminated the Grand Junction land from the list of relocation sites, apparently because the Tabeguache group refused to accept it.

In compliance with orders from U.S. officials, the White Rivers and other Northern Utes except the Tabeguaches assembled near Grand Junction in spring 1881 for relocation. The military then accompanied them to Utah, to what later became the Consolidated Uintah-Ouray Reservation. The Tabeguaches accepted relocation to Utah later the same year.

A number of Utes who took part in the final treaty negotiations met death in bizarre ways. For example, Captain Jack resisted arrest in 1882 on suspicion of horse theft and died when the U.S. Army lobbed howitzer shells into his dwelling. Tabeguache Chief Piah took his own life in 1888.

Not until the 1940s did the Federal justice system produce a monetary formula to compensate the Utes for the millions of Colorado acres taken from them as a result of the 1880 relocation agreement. Former sheep rancher Elmer Bair of Carbondale, who was familiar with both Utah and Colorado lands, commented in 1994 on the Ute relocations. Had the miners and settlers been forced onto the lands that the United States gave the Native Americans, they would have starved to death, he said.

III

MINING SPURS DEVELOPMENT

Mining booms piloted the development of Colorado. The often feverish quest for precious metals lured prospectors into the Glenwood Canyon vicinity before the Utes relinquished the lands involved. Ranchers, farmers, merchants, town planners, gamblers, and prostitutes followed closely on the miners' heels, precipitating formation of the first formal and informal settlements in and near the canyon. Early settlements ranged from ranches to organized townsites.

GRAND SPRINGS AND DEFIANCE BECOME GLENWOOD SPRINGS

Captain Richard Sopris led a prospecting and surveying expedition to this area of hot springs and sunshine in 1860. Illness struck Sopris, and members of the party took him to the site of today's hot springs complex in Glenwood Springs for therapy. At that time, the river flowed in two channels there, and the group spent a week on the island between the channels. Sopris named the place Grand Springs.

Sunlight and shadow on Colorado River, Glenwood Canyon.
Date unknown.

James M. Landis visited the area in 1878 and found a
promising site for a ranch at the junction of the Grand (Colorado) and Roaring Fork rivers. The next year, he filed for
squatters rights on 160 acres and built a cabin there.

At that point in time, development of the future Glenwood
Springs became closely related to the rise and fall of Carbonate

City to the north and the attempted development of Defiance City to the northeast.

Silver Attracts Crowd

The White River Plateau north of Glenwood Canyon drew a share of attention from prospectors who combed the mountains in search of precious metals in the late 1870s and early 1880s. A small number of Leadville prospectors in 1878 found rock outcroppings they associated with carbonates — ores of silver and lead — about 15 miles north of Grand Springs near the 10,785-foot elevation. The men soon left to spend the winter at Leadville.

Returning to their area of interest in spring 1879, the men had the company of a crowd of prospectors who hoped to grasp a share of the anticipated riches. Several miles from the original discovery, prospectors built a log blockhouse for use in the event of Indian attack. They called the crude fortification Fort Defiance.

With the departure of the Utes in spring 1881, business people and more prospectors investigated the area. They filed hundreds of mining claims during the next couple of years. Thousands of people camped on the plateau north of Glenwood Canyon, especially between Fort Defiance and the origins of Grizzly and No Name creeks.

French Creek, which joined the Colorado River in the canyon, received its name as a result of disagreement involving early prospectors. A Frenchman and two other men had a camp at the creek in the winter of 1880-1881. After quarreling with his companions, the Frenchman left, moved downstream, and built his own cabin. He remained there in self-imposed exile for some time, even after his former friends resumed their prospecting in spring.

Defiance Promoted, Then Moved

A party of Leadville men who arrived in the Fort Defiance area in April 1880 established a town company. They prepared a map of their planned 640-acre Defiance development situated about six miles northeast of Grand Springs. The site near Wagon Gulch extended across Glenwood Canyon, embracing lands above the north and south rims. Those involved in the project were W. M. Bell, Henry Blake, John C. Blake, Rufus Coates, D. Cole, C. C. Davis, James M. Landis, Joseph Long, and H. W. Shannon. An advertisement in a Leadville newspaper predicted a population of 5,000 "before fall" for this "elysium of the New West" located on a high plateau. The ad offered a limited number of free lots to the first settlers who would agree to make their homes in the community.

Acceptance of the offer was so poor that no development of any importance took place on the site. Other men joined some of the original backers in the 1882 formation of the Defiance Town and Land Company, and they moved the location of the planned community six miles southwest to Grand Springs. The backers included H. P. Bennett, John Blake, Frank Enzensperger, William Gelder, and Isaac Cooper. The latter had been involved in Colorado mining ventures since 1875. He had obtained relief from his ailments in the hot springs, and in 1882 he bought the Landis ranch for possible resort development.

According to U.S. Land Office records, Deputy Surveyor W. A. Illsley surveyed a Defiance Townsite, which was then in Summit County, in performance of a contract dated November 23, 1882, and the General Land Office received his diagram of the site near year's end. Albert Johnson, Surveyor General for Colorado, approved the diagram on January 16, 1883. The town company received a patent on the townsite of Defiance, Patent 853, dated April 25, 1883.

Carbonate City Rivals Defiance

Circumstances in 1883 favored efforts to organize the town of Carbonate City, also called Carbonateville and simply Car-

Opposite Page: Part of Defiance Townsite plat approved by U.S. Surveyor General's Office, Denver, January 16, 1883.

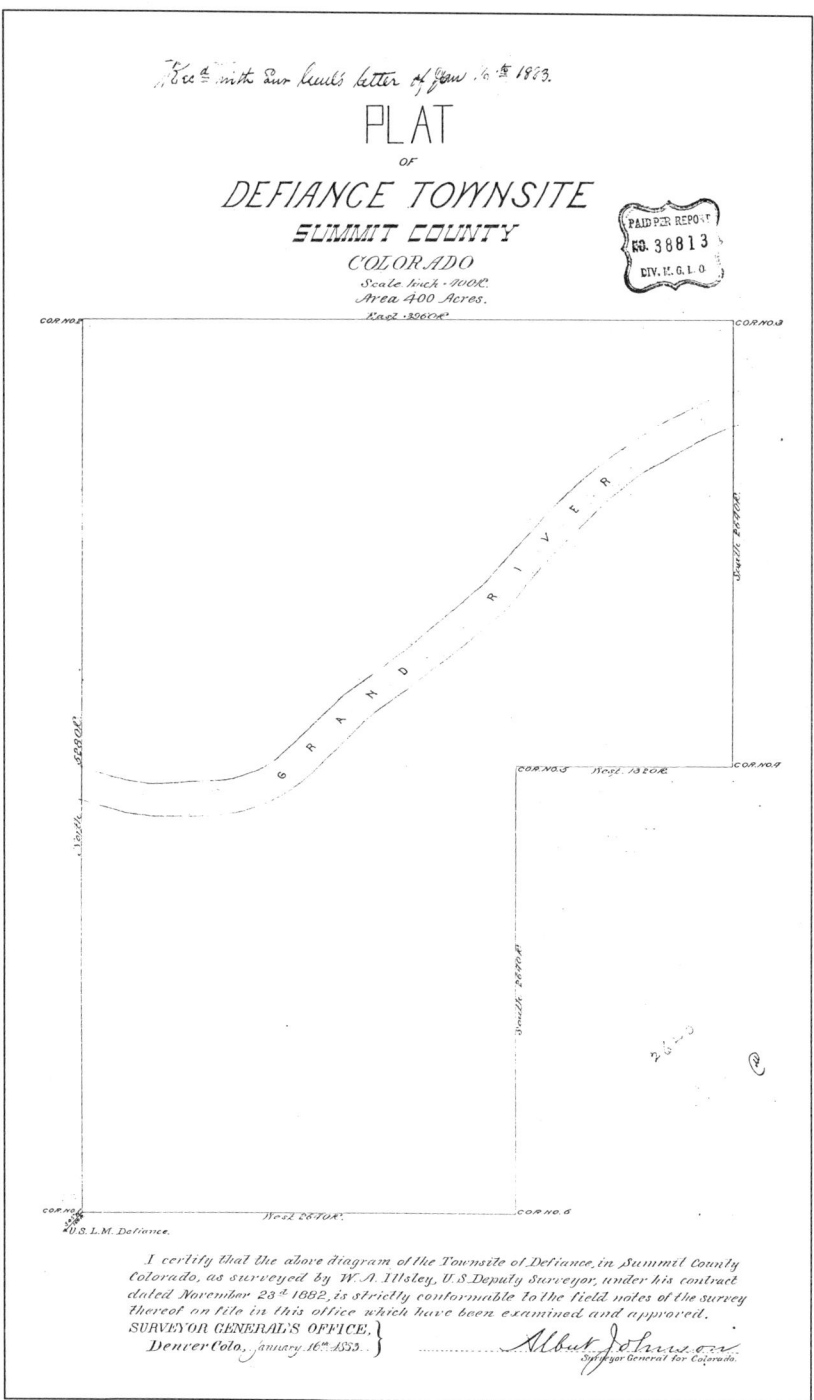

Rec.d with Sur Genl's letter of Jan. 16th 1883.

PLAT
OF
DEFIANCE TOWNSITE
SUMMIT COUNTY
COLORADO
Scale 1 inch · 400.R.
Area 400 Acres.

COR.NO.2   East 3960.R.   COR.NO.3

G R A N D   R I V E R

South 2640.R.

South 3520.R.

North 3520.R.

COR.NO.5   West 1320.R.   COR.NO.4

South 2640.R.

COR.NO.1   West 2640.R.   COR.NO.6

U.S.L.M. Defiance.

I certify that the above diagram of the Townsite of Defiance, in Summit County Colorado, as surveyed by W.A. Illsley, U.S.Deputy Surveyor, under his contract dated November 23.d 1882, is strictly conformable to the field notes of the survey thereof on file in this office which have been examined and approved.
SURVEYOR GENERAL'S OFFICE,
Denver Colo, January 16th 1883.

Albert Johnson
Surveyor General for Colorado.

bonate, on the plateau at the place of the original silver discovery of 1878. The state legislature carved land from Summit County to create the new County of Garfield, and Carbonate received the designation as county seat. First official papers filed there were documents establishing the Carbonate town company. On April 5, town organizers filed a plat of the proposed development with the U.S. Land Office.

Miners labored to dig shafts in order to establish new claims or retain existing mineral rights, but most of the diggings never progressed beyond the 50-foot level. Mining laws required the expenditure of a certain amount of work before filing claims and additional improvements each year to retain mining rights. Failing to encounter marketable ore, miners often hoped to sell their properties, and they performed just enough work to satisfy the laws while seeking buyers. The average sales price of claims around Carbonate was then close to $1,000.

Mining laws also contained provisions allowing miners to patent their claims, thereby acquiring title to the land and eliminating the annual improvement requirement. But the patent process required additional expenditures of time, money, and effort. Few Carbonate-area claims reached that stage.

Even when a miner had rich ore in sight, it was very difficult for him to operate profitably. The biggest problems were an absence of effective, local facilities for ore processing and the high cost of hauling ores by burro and wagon to distant plants. While Carbonate-area ore deposits proved small and generally of low grade, miners there apparently had some potentially profitable ore, because they made a number of shipments to Leadville and Redcliff smelters.

Development of the 160-acre townsite was similarly dull. It consisted of a store or saloon, post office building, about 15 log dwellings, and a nearby sawmill. Brutal weather exacerbated the community's problems. Using the height of tree stumps as a guide, one man later determined that the snow had been eight to twelve feet deep when persistent miners felled trees at the townsite.

Accurate population figures were difficult to obtain. Some miners lived in huts or tents on or near the townsite, while others sought the shelter of shaft houses on their claims. At the beginning of June 1883, there were about 100 men at the townsite proper. During four years at the height of the boom, between 2,000 and 5,000 people camped in that general area.

Defiance Becomes Glenwood Springs; Carbonate Fades

As was the case with many Colorado settlements, early residents of Defiance, at the confluence of the Colorado and Roaring Fork rivers, used tents, dugouts, and cabins as temporary shelters for their homes and businesses while awaiting supplies for construction of more appropriate quarters. Supplies were costly and slow to arrive because of difficulty in freighting them across the mountains on burros and horse-drawn wagons.

Fred A. Barlow started his Grand Springs Hotel in a large tent that also served as the town's first post office. The name of that post office, established on June 25, 1883 to serve the Defiance area, was Barlow. Mr. Barlow's wife Ella reportedly was the postmistress. A notice in the regular postal bulletin issued by the Post Office Department listed the July 28 appointment of a Caroline E. Barlow as postmistress.

Because Isaac Cooper's wife Sarah disliked the name Defiance, town fathers in 1883 changed the name. They chose the name Glenwood Springs in honor of Sarah's home town of Glenwood, Iowa.

The beneficent circumstances that just a few months earlier had given nearby Carbonate a seemingly bright future vanished in late 1883 and assured the settlement's rapid demise. Garfield County commissioners dismissed County Clerk and Recorder C. A. McBrairty in October for dereliction of duty. They suspected him of involvement in a scheme to increase the sales of townsite lots in Carbonate by augmenting assay samples of Carbonate-area ores with rich samples from the mines of Leadville.

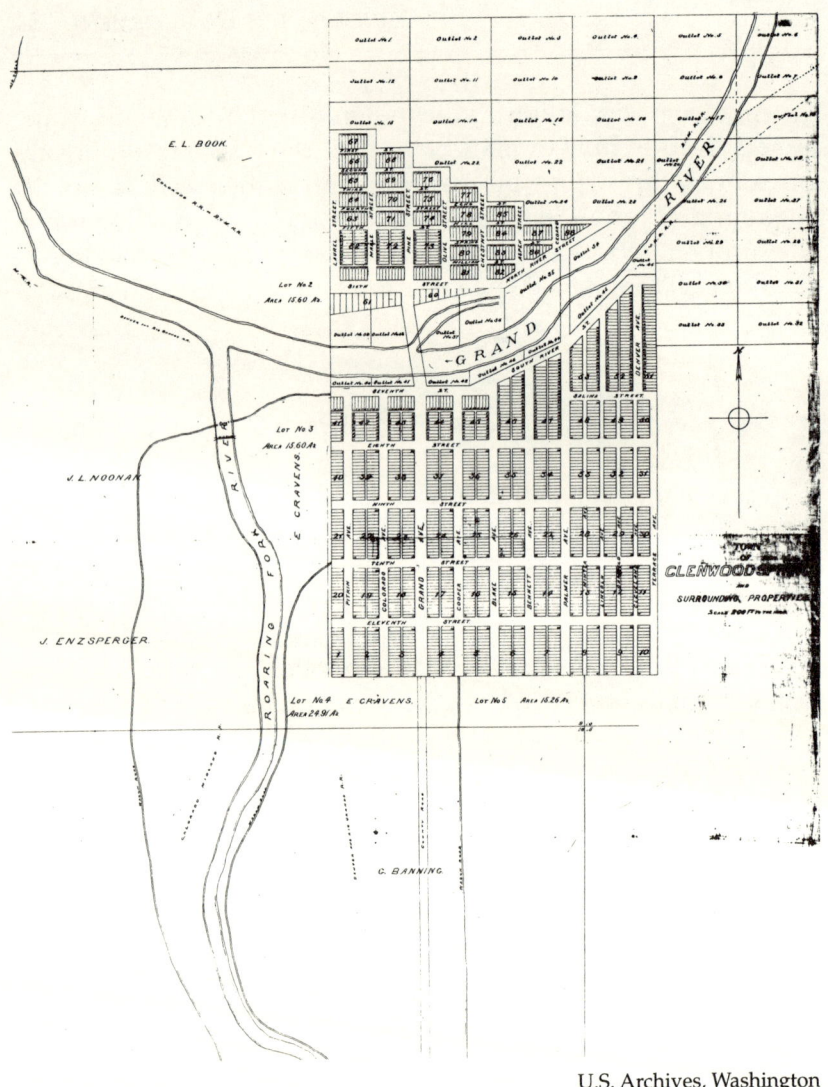

Glenwood Springs Townsite.

In the November election, Garfield County voters selected Glenwood Springs as the permanent seat of county government, and Carbonate's brief existence was essentially over before the end of 1883.

In 1884, the name of the Barlow Post Office changed and finally matched the name of the town in which it operated. The name changed officially to Glenwood Springs on March 28, according to Bauer and others in *Colorado Postal History*.

Glenwood's first newspapers went to press in 1885. They were the *Glenwood Echo*, with James L. Riland as editor, and *The Ute Chief* with J. S. and W. J. Reid. History of today's *Glenwood Post* began with the 1898 debut of an A. J. Dickson paper of the same name.

Glenwood Springs Incorporates

Desiring to replace the government organized by the town company and institute a municipal structure under Colorado statutes, Glenwood citizens began an incorporation effort. Garfield County Court in late July 1885 received a petition signed by 41 residents requesting incorporation of Glenwood Springs as a municipality. Supporting the request, according to records of the Colorado Secretary of State, were a description and plat of the 640-acre area to be incorporated and Frank Enzensperger's affidavit stating that some 400 people live within the boundaries of the proposed municipality. The qualified electors in the affected area voted in favor of the proposal in August. Glenwood's population grew to 700 in the next year.

Holliday Comes to Town

Glenwood Springs hosted a wide variety of people right from the start — the unknown, the famous, and the infamous. In the latter category was John Henry Holliday, better known as Doc. Holliday was a dentist, but his reputation stemmed primarily from his gambling, drinking, and a trail of gunslinging confrontations.

Among various writings concerning Doc Holliday, the number of deaths attributed to him ranged between 8 and 25.

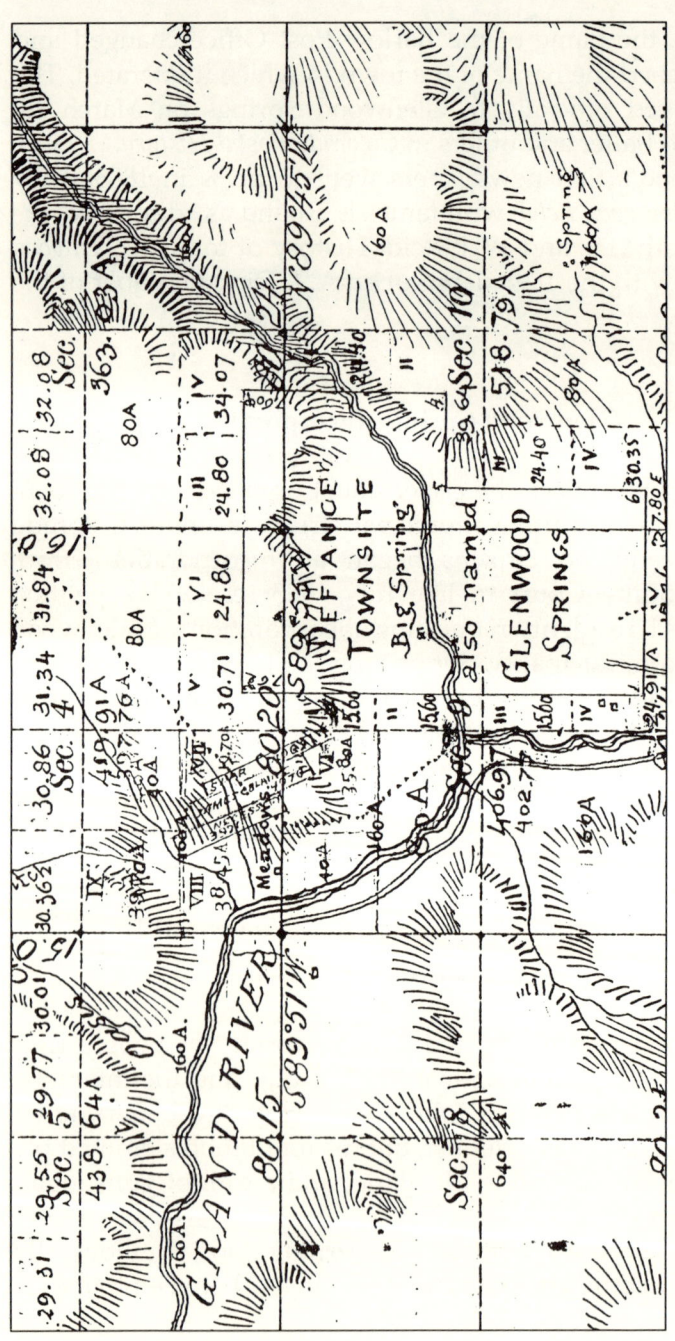

Part of an 1880s survey diagram showing Defiance/Glenwood Springs Townsite.

John Henry
(Doc) Holliday.

Frontier Historical Museum, Glenwood Springs, Colorado

Frontier Historical Society in Glenwood Springs settled on a tentative figure of 12. Holliday became known as "the deadly dentist."

When Holliday came to Glenwood in 1887, there were at least 20 saloons within two blocks in the main business district. But Holliday's move to Glenwood was an act of desperation beyond a desire for drinking and gambling. Holliday came in hopes of effecting a cure for his tuberculosis. He came to town in May, and death overtook him in his bed at Hotel Glenwood on November eighth, reportedly after he drank a glass of whiskey. He was 35.

Saloonkeepers and their customers donated money to pay for Holliday's grave. Burial took place in Linwood Cemetery in

Glenwood Springs. The grave finally received a stone marker in 1958.

Glenwood Springs in 1987 observed the 100th anniversary of Holliday's death with dancing, country/western music, dancehall girls, staging of a shootout, and a night of poker games at Hotel Denver. The belated wake was a benefit for Frontier Historical Society.

Rails Give Glenwood a Boost

Railroads meant faster, less expensive delivery of supplies for home and business, opened up a viable conduit for marketing of an area's own products, and provided easier access for investors, immigrants, and tourists. With some 170 miles of mountainous terrain between Glenwood Springs and Denver, Glenwood needed rails in order to grow and prosper. Glenwood was doubly fortunate. Rails came to town from two railroads. Rio Grande rolled into Glenwood from the east via the canyon, and Colorado Midland arrived later from the south.

As Rio Grande construction neared Glenwood, the community's population increased with more opportunists hoping to take advantage of the increased traffic the trains would bring.

Excitement intensified when construction crews pounded in the final spikes to bring the Rio Grande line into town. The school interrupted its schedule, allowing the children to join many townsfolk at the scene of this important event.

No Glenwood Springs celebration has surpassed the raucous exuberance accompanying the 1887 arrival of the first train. With O. B. Gutshall at the throttle of Number 187, the lead locomotive, it arrived on the evening of October 5. Aboard the 20-car special were hundreds of dignitaries. The guest list included Colorado Governor Alva Adams and his entourage, Rio Grande President David H. Moffat, member of the board W. S. Cheesman, the road's counsel E. O. Wolcott, and Glenwood Springs pioneer Isaac Cooper.

Crowds of cheering townspeople turned out for the occasion. The celebration was bright and loud. Residents lighted

Frontier Historical Museum, Glenwood Springs, Colorado

First train in Glenwood Springs, a Rio Grande special, Oct. 5, 1887.

candles in front of their homes. There were bonfires, fireworks, detonations of Giant Powder, speeches, and music by a brass band. For invited guests, there was a banquet.

The Colorado Midland's first train entered Glenwood Springs on December 12, 1887. There was a celebration of its arrival, but it was only a shadow of the great welcome accorded the earlier debut of the Rio Grande. Townspeople had spent their money, time, and enthusiasm on the previous festivities, and an air of sadness hung over the town because of the recent death of town father Isaac Cooper. He died in Hotel Glenwood on December 2 at age 48. Burial took place in Riverside Cemetery, Denver.

Even after the arrival of the railroads, stagecoaches continued their runs. Lines serving Glenwood included the Kit Carson, Barlow & Sanderson, and the Western Stage Company. Stages continued service to the little communities and remote resorts beyond the reach of rails well into the 20th century, even after the advent of horseless carriages. Meantime, the two railroads provided many jobs and were vital factors in attracting tourists. Word of the scenic rail rides, Glenwood's hot springs and vapor caves, and the excellent, nearby fishing and hunting soon spread worldwide and made the Glenwood Springs area an alluring destination for vacationers. Regular, roundtrip fares for passengers between Glenwood Springs and Denver were $25.70 on both railroads around 1891.

Relations Cordial Between Utes, Townspeople

Both before and after the Ute relocation, relations between Utes and settlers in the Glenwood vicinity could be described as friendly. After Chief Ouray's 1880 death, his widow Chipeta sought relief of her rheumatism in the hot springs. For years, a group of Utes, including Chief Colorow, made annual visits to Glenwood. In her book *Colorow*, Lena M. Urquhart wrote of her personal friend Eleanora Malaby who came to Glenwood in 1885. Eleanora and her husband Perry invited the Utes into their home every year until members of the tribe ended their treks from the reservation.

In his last years, Chief Colorow spent much time in Glenwood Springs. Wearing a blanket, moccasins, and a tall "plug" hat made of black silk, he sat beside the hot springs and drew the attention of tourists. His last visit took place in the summer of 1887. At that time, he showed the effects of age — poor hearing and posture, senility, depression, and a five-foot, eight-inch frame burdened by 275 pounds.

In a book concerning medical practice in early Colorado, Doctor Robert H. Shikes wrote that Colorow suffered from dropsy (abnormal accumulation of fluids) and ascites (dropsy of the abdomen), but "his problem may actually have been alcohol cirrhosis." A doctor removed the fluid on a number of occasions. Colorow later tried the procedure himself. In the process, his unsterilized knife damaged the intestine, peritonitis developed, and death soon occurred.

A few hours before his December 1888 death, Colorow reportedly reiterated a charge that forgery had forced his people to relinquish their lands. Perhaps *bribery* would have been a better choice of words. When Utes balked at signing the 1880 relocation agreement, a government representative paid two dollars to each man who would sign, according to the writings of Sidney Jocknick.

RESORTS DEVELOPED

Of the hot springs that rose along the Colorado River at Glenwood, those in the northeast part of town became the most highly developed and most famous. Smaller resort and health developments appeared around other springs in and near the town at various times and with varying degrees of longevity.

The springs reach the surface through faults in the Belden Formation shales. The faulting results from long-ago upward tilting of the shales where they rest against the south end of the White River Plateau.

While they are not the hottest in Colorado, the springs at Glenwood discharge water at a higher rate than any other group in the state. As a group, these springs produce 3,000 gallons per minute at temperatures between 106 and 125 degrees. Heating of the water and enhancement of its mineral content take place miles away and probably result from hot gases rising from deep masses of rock that retain the heat of ancient volcanic activity.

George Allan Collection, Colorado Historical Society 16664

The pool complex, Glenwood Springs, May 1898.

The Big Pool and Hotel Colorado

Walter B. Devereux fostered the formation of the Colorado Land and Improvement Company in 1887. After reorganization, the firm became the Glenwood Hot Springs Company. Stockholders included Walter Devereux, his brothers Henry and Horace, J. R. Busk of New York, and James J. Hagerman of Colorado Springs. Those men, singly or with others, were good organizers with ability to raise capital and were leading forces in development of Glenwood Springs. Among their projects were railroads, coal mines, banks, and the facilities that became the town's most famous resort complex — the Vapor Caves, a large swimming pool, a fine bath house and lodge designed to appeal to the rich and famous, and the elegant six-floor Hotel Colorado. The hot springs company named Theodore von Rosenberg as architect and engineer to lead the design and construction of the pool and hotel.

The pool was 500 feet long, 100 feet wide, and 3.5 to 5.5 feet deep — the largest naturally heated, outdoor mineral pool in the world. It opened in 1888, and the bath house, lodge, and casino went into service in 1890. Cost of the pool, bath house, a walkway and access road, and grooming of the surroundings came to $400,000.

The place was popular with local people and visitors as well. Aspen-area residents boarded excursion trains that carried them the 42 miles to Glenwood for evenings at the pool. Miners were in the habit of taking a bath and washing their laundry at the same time, and the trains became known as "laundry trains." The excursions left Aspen at six o'clock and returned about four hours later. Roundtrip fare of two dollars included admission to the big pool.

Around that time, modest ladies clad in the customary woolen bathing suits and stockings could bathe in sunken tubs beneath the bath house. The bath house staff included a resident physician.

Use of the sunken tubs ended long ago. And a number of other changes occurred since then. According to the *Glenwood*

Denver Public Library Western Collection

Bath house, lodge, and swimming pool, Glenwood Springs circa 1900.

Post, Frank Kistler, who had acquired the pool complex in 1937, sold the springs, lodge, and pool in 1956 to Glenwood Hot Springs Lodge and Pool Inc., a closed corporation owned by 22 Glenwood Springs businessmen. At the time of the sale, the complex included the main lodge with 60 guest rooms, 2 chalet-style motels, a restaurant, an enclosed promenade, some private cabanas, a therapy center, and the pool itself. The new owners completed a modernization that included a new bath house made of concrete blocks and reconstruction of the pool in 1960.

In a 1977 news release, the pool corporation reported on progress of an expansion that included "enlarged bath house facilities, additional sunbathing area, new kiddie pool, and new maintenance building," and in 1994 came the completion of an ambitious restoration of the original bath house. The historic bath house, made of red sandstone, now contains the corporate offices as well as facilities for an athletic club.

Water from these springs is between 111 and 124 degrees as it emerges from the ground. To lower the temperature to a level suitable for swimming, the pool's intake system includes a cold-water source. Temperature in the small pool hovers around 104 degrees, some 14 degrees warmer than its giant neighbor. There is a change of water in the large pool every six hours. Within the same period of time, water in the small pool changes three times. The facilities are lighted at night and are open all year.

Completion of the 250-room Hotel Colorado came in 1893 at a cost of $850,000. It opened to the public on June 10. Rio Grande and Colorado Midland both scheduled special trains for the grand opening. Events included a polo match between Glenwood Springs and Colorado Springs teams. Swimmers enjoyed free admission to the hot springs pool. While guests attended a grand ball in the hotel, other revelers danced outside on Grand Avenue.

The hotel, patterned after the Villa de Midas in Italy, hosted many famous people during its long history. Among them were Presidents Theodore Roosevelt and William Howard Taft, actor Tom Mix, Buffalo Bill Cody, and gangster Al Capone.

President Theodore Roosevelt visited the Glenwood Springs area a number of times, but his hunting trip of mid April 1905 was the most auspicious and had the greatest, apparent impact on the nation. The well-publicized trip afforded the President an opportunity to further his views on conservation. The visit also inspired creation of the teddybear and drew additional attention to the multifaceted appeal of the Glenwood area. Hotel Colorado served as the White House during Roosevelt's visit.

Detroit Photographic Company

Part of Glenwood Springs around 1900.

The President and his party arrived on the tracks of the Midland. They bagged three lynx and ten Black Bears during the ensuing hunt. Laid out on the shrubbery at Hotel Colorado, one particularly large bear drew the attention of reporters as well as Roosevelt's daughter Alice. The teenager commented that she would name that animal "Teddy's bear." Entrepreneurs rushed to manufacture toy versions of the bear, triggering the nation's long-standing infatuation with teddy-bears.

Glenwood decorated its streets and extended a hearty welcome to Roosevelt. Upon his return to Hotel Colorado after the

Denver Public Library Western Collection

Part of Glenwood Springs around 1900.

hunt, the President twice appeared and spoke briefly to the assembled crowds. He thanked them for the warm welcome. He mingled with the crowds and shook hands. He spent some time walking the streets and shaking more hands. When the President departed in early May, he rode the Rio Grande route eastward. The lead locomotive on his train was No. 720, first on that route to use an electrically powered headlight.

Ownership of Hotel Colorado changed a number of times through the years. During World War II, the Federal Government took over the facilities for use as a recuperation hospital for U.S. Navy personnel.

Frontier Historical Museum, Glenwood Springs, Colorado

President Theodore Roosevelt addressed crowd from
Hotel Colorado balcony, 1905.

In the 1960s, owner Joseph W. Vittum converted some of
the upper rooms into apartments and made some space on
lower floors available for lease as offices.

A celebration of the hotel's 100th anniversary took place in
1993. It featured tours of the building, a polo championship,
historical exhibits and 1890s attire, music, and dance.

Townspeople Support Polo

Walter B. Devereux, his brothers Horace K. and James H.,
Steve Baxter, and other townspeople organized a polo and rac-
ing association and built a polo field, race track, grandstand,
and clubhouse south of town beside what is now the Roaring
Fork Subdivision. Harvey Lyle, an experienced player, was

apparently the principal motivator in efforts to establish the sport in Glenwood. Experienced players in town were few, too few for completion of an opposition team. The association solved that problem by recruiting cowboys and other horsemen and familiarizing them with the game.

Players took to the field for the first game in 1890. The polo competition and horse races were among the few diversions available to townsfolk, and attendance was excellent.

Glenwood's regular participation in polo competition ended following the 1912 death of Harvey Lyle, and the polo grounds became a golf course after World War I.

The Star and Hotel Denver

Hotel Denver, in the business district at 402 Seventh Street across the river from Hotel Colorado, began as the Denver Rooms, operated by Art Kendrick above a grocery store. When Kendrick purchased the building, it became Hotel Denver. Meantime, Henry Bosco remodeled a nearby building and established the Star Hotel. Both men then expanded their hostelries. Bosco in 1908 hired his 15-year-old nephew Marcus (Mike) Bosco, a native of northern Italy, and put him to work in the Star.

Following a late 1930s fire at Hotel Denver, Henry purchased the Denver. In rebuilding it, he combined it with the Star. With this addition and some remodeling over the years, the number of guest rooms in Hotel Denver varied; the maximum number was round 95. In 1947, Henry's heirs sold the properties to Mike Bosco and Mike's son Henry.

Hotel Glenwood

An establishment called the Colorado Hotel appeared at Eighth and Grand about 1883. Two years later, it made way for Hotel Glenwood, which hosted such luminaries as Doc Holliday and Baby Doe and H. A. W. Tabor. Five people died there in 1945 when fire leveled the building.

W. H. Jackson photo

Part of Glenwood Springs, late 1800s.

The St. James/St. Joseph/Grand

Fred Barlow started the St. James Hotel in 1883 at Eighth and Cooper. Before long, construction of Hotel Yampa took place in front of the St. James. In 1899, the Sisters of Mercy

Denver Public Library Western Collection

bought the St. James and converted it to St. Joseph Sanitorium and Hotel. The venture failed, and the manager of Hotel Glenwood acquired the property and operated it as an upper-class establishment called the Grand Hotel. But the building had structural problems which resulted in its condemnation and demolition in 1934.

W. H. Jackson photo   Denver Public Library Western Collection

Part of Glenwood Springs between 1890 and 1899.

Other Accommodations Plentiful

Around 1900, in addition to accommodations available at Glenwood Springs hotels, cottages provided around 125 rooms, and homeowners also rented space to tourists. Rates ranged from a low of about one dollar per day in a private home to a high of six dollars at Hotel Colorado.

Glenwood Springs was the jumping-off spot for such attractions as Deep and Trappers lakes. There were lodges at both of those popular destinations.

LOOKING AT 20TH CENTURY HAPPENINGS

Glenwood Springs in the 20th century matured from a town to a city. The Strawberry festival gained momentum. One of the settlement's most influential developers died. The ski industry evolved, mining in the region brought not only favors but pains, and nature sparked a heartbreaking tragedy. On balance, population growth continued, and Glenwood shared the beginnings of urbanization with other areas of the Western Slope.

Festival Becomes Perennial Event

Glenwood Springs in 1898 inaugurated what would become the state's oldest, continuing, civic festival. It began as Strawberry *Day* and evolved to Strawberry *Days* as the scope of the June celebration stretched well beyond the hallmark feast of strawberries and cake. In addition to special attractions that varied from year to year, the festival often included parades, tournaments, arts and crafts fairs, rodeos, and swimsuit and fashion competitions.

Devereux Stricken

The man responsible for so much of Glenwood's early development returned eventually to his mining roots. Walter Devereux resumed his career as a mining engineer, operating from a New York City office. On occasion, he returned to Glenwood for fishing and hunting. After such a trip in 1905, a stroke forced his retirement. He died in California on November 19, 1934.

Town Achieves City Status

The 1910 census showed Glenwood Springs with a population of 2,019. That entitled the town to become a City of the Second Class. Governor John F. Shafroth issued an executive order "Proclaiming Town of Glenwood Springs . . . a City of the Second Class" on January 29, 1912. On February 2, Colorado Secretary of State James B. Pearce sent a "Certificate of Notice of Change" to Glenwood Mayor E. C. Drach, according to records of the Colorado Secretary of State. Copies of the notice went to a Denver newspaper and *The Avalanche* in Glenwood Springs with orders for publication.

In November 1947, Glenwood voters elected a city council to complete the adoption of a city council-city manager form of government.

Mining Influences Fates, Fortunes

Glenwood Springs has never been strictly a mining town. From the start, it has been more diversified than that. Nevertheless, it has been heavily influenced by the vagaries of the mining industry. Town father Walter Devereux, for instance, came from a mining background. Glenwood development arose partly from the failed promise of Carbonate, when miners sought survival in other fields — ranches, farms, retail businesses, and resort operations. Early visitors included Aspen-area miners riding the trains to Glenwood for weekly bathing and laundry sessions. Wealthy foreigners sojourned in Glenwood, attracted by polo, mineral waters, and business opportunities that included Colorado mines. There was development of coal deposits to the south. Later came attempts to unlock alluring but repeatedly elusive wealth from massive deposits of oil shale toward the west.

Glenwood noted a population increase from 1,350 in 1900 to a 1960 count of 3,637. Kingpins of the economy in the 1960s were farming, ranching, and tourism. Factors of lesser importance were the coal mining and some activity in connection with silver and marble to the south, limestone processing, and timber operations.

Development of oil shale operations, skiing, highway construction, and modernization of facilities for handling of railroad freight produced a period of growth and change that began in the 1960s and expanded into a major boom before the shale industry crashed in the early 1980s. Glenwood Springs underwent changes that included construction of new build-ings and remodeling of old structures. There were new homes, a new building for the post office and other federal agencies, expansion of Valley View Hospital, a combination city hall and fire station, and extension of the city limits through annexation.

Meantime, the escalating popularity of skiing also had its effects. Glenwood experienced an early association with this activity. During World War II, members of the Army's Tenth Mountain Division received specialized training in skiing and other skills in preparation for cold-weather action overseas. Training centered in the Camp Hale area on Tennessee Pass, but the troops practiced skiing in other areas of the mountains as well. While these men underwent training, some of their fami-lies lived in Glenwood Springs. The troops came to Glenwood to visit their families and to spend some time in recreational skiing in the area.

A small ski development opened just south of the city on Red Mountain in 1966. And Ski Sunlight, at Four Mile Creek, began operation in the 1966-1967 season. With Sunlight only 12 miles to the south, Aspen about 40 miles away, and Vail about 60, combination rates for lodging, skiing, and swimming proved popular and strengthened Glenwood's position as a year-round resort.

Oil Success Perennially Elusive

Sporadic endeavors aimed at development of vast oil shale deposits 30 to 40 miles west of Glenwood Springs placed the city on an economic roller coaster beginning in the 1920s. But nothing equalled the scale and impact of the massive projects launched in the 1970s in efforts to decrease the nation's depen-dence on oil imports. Communities from Glenwood Springs to Grand Junction experienced a boom as thousands of workers moved in to develop shale mines and the plants to extract the oil. Exxon, Gulf, Mobil, Occidental, Unocal, and some smaller

Loretta B. Schader

Above: Eastbound along horseshoe bend, U.S. 6 & 24, east side of Glenwood Springs, October 1971. Bend bypassed in 1960s by construction through twin tunnels from Glenwood Springs to No Name. *Below:* On bypassed U.S. 6 & 24 segment at horseshoe bend, June 1977.

Conrad F. Schader

firms launched projects. Preparations began for housing and business establishments that would be necessary for thousands of permanent employees once the shale industry reached the production stage.

Falling oil prices caused abandonment, indefinite suspension, or severe contraction of one project after another, until the only full-scale effort still underway by a major oil company was the project by Unocal Corporation. The Unocal plant managed to start oil production but suspended operation in 1991.

Congress soon dealt the staggering industry a decisive blow. Lawmakers in 1985 abolished the Synthetic Fuels Corporation it had created five years earlier to help finance development of synthetic fuels.

After a brief slide backward, growth resumed strongly despite the oil shale bust. Bolstered by hundreds of people working on highway construction for extended periods of time and thousands of newcomers fleeing congested metropolitan areas of the United States, it followed the march of I-70 construction across the state and delivered urbanization to the Western Slope at least a decade before the 1992 completion of the highway's final link in Glenwood Canyon.

The 1960 census counted 3,637 people in Glenwood Springs. By 1982, the population was about 4,600. By 1994, with some 66 percent of Coloradans residing along the I-70 corridor between Denver and Grand Junction, and with heavy, transcontinental traffic, parts of I-70 already were inadequate for peak-period traffic.

It would be wrong to characterize recent Glenwood Springs history strictly in terms of population and the resilience of the economy, for the area has experienced some tragic events whose effects have transcended economic considerations.

Explosions, Fire Prove Deadly

Nine miners lost their lives in December 1965 when a methane explosion rocked a coal mine in the vicinity of Redstone, thirty miles southwest of Glenwood Springs. In April

1981, 15 miners died when another methane blast struck the Mid-Continent Resources operation. The victims were as far as 7,200 feet into a mountain and 2,000 feet beneath the surface in the Dutch Creek Mine No. 1. According to newspaper accounts, six of the dead were residents of Glenwood Springs. Dutch Creek Mine No. 1 closed permanently in January 1991. Work soon began on projects to seal the mine and reclaim the nearby lands.

A propane explosion destroyed the Rocky Mountain Natural Gas Company building in Glenwood in December 1985. Twelve people died.

One of the deadliest wildfires in U.S. history swept the rugged slopes of Storm King Mountain, just west of Glenwood Springs, in 1994.* Though there was disagreement over the day the fire became evident, it was sometime over the long Fourth of July weekend.

It was a hot, dry summer; vegetation was the driest it had been in two decades. Around July 2, a Saturday, lightning ignited a small fire on the mountain about five miles west of Glenwood Springs. Firefighters checked the area from an airplane on Monday but reported only the smoldering of an inactive fire, and they flew onward to battle a couple of serious fires elsewhere in Colorado.

By Wednesday afternoon, firefighters — 40 from the Bureau of Land Management and 30 volunteers from departments at Carbondale, Glenwood Springs, and Silt — were on the scene at Storm King Mountain. Suddenly, erratic 50-mile-per-hour winds whipped the remnants of that small fire into a raging inferno that engulfed 2,400 acres of juniper, scrub oak, and piñon within two hours. The use of tanker planes to drop fire retardant was impossible because of winds. Speeding on the brutally shifting winds, flames pursued 52 firefighters and killed 14 of them. The victims were 10 men and 4 women, all of them members of elite, highly trained helitack, smoke jumper,

---

* This account is based on press reports published during and after the fire.

and hot shot units. Rich Tyler, a helitack foreman, lived in Pal-
isade, Colorado. The other 13 were from Montana, Idaho, and
Oregon.

Smoke darkened the sky. Flames swept southward, coming
within 12 feet of I-70 and threatening West Glenwood as the
powerful winds brought the onslaught within 1,500 feet of a
mall and endangered a subdivision. But another change in
wind turned the fire away and spared both West Glenwood
and Glenwood Springs. Flames failed to reach any homes.

The blaze raged into mid July. Efforts involving 7 tanker
planes, 5 helicopters, and 452 people finally controlled it on
July 16 and extinguished it by August 5.

Condolences filled mailboxes of the victims' families. Contributions poured into a benefit fund, enough to give $30,000 to
each family.

Heavy rain unleashed an avalanche from the denuded
slopes of Storm King on a Thursday night in September. Mud
and debris slid across I-70, buried five cars, and injured two
people. Working day and night, highway crews cleared one
lane in each direction on Friday afternoon. Removal of the
unwieldy mass from the remaining lanes required another two
days.

Using a helicopter, the Bureau of Land Management later
dropped thousands of pounds of seeds on the mountain in an
attempt to re-establish vegetation and stabilize the soil. The
attempt was successful.

In a project spearheaded by Bob Mackey, father of fire victim Don Mackey, 80 cadets from the Air Force Academy in
April 1995 joined other volunteers to remove debris and put up
signs along a one-mile interpretive trail built earlier by volunteers on Storm King Mountain in memory of the grim battle.
They set 14 small crosses in concrete, each granite cross bearing
the name of a firefighter.

A year after the deaths, about 2,000 spectators, survivors,
and relatives and friends of the firefighters attended the dedication of a monument in Glenwood's Two Rivers Park. The monument honored the 14 who died and 35 who escaped the

Part of a large photograph of Glenwood Springs, 1948.

inferno's sudden advance. On the same day, residents of Canyon Creek Estates subdivision, threatened for a time, dedicated their own memorial — 14 boulders and plaques at the subdivision entrance.

Relatives and friends of the firefighters still speak of the friendships that developed among them and of their appreciation of the sympathetic response they received from the people of Glenwood Springs during and after the ordeal.

Looking at Today's Glenwood Springs

In 1995, population of Glenwood Springs approached the 7,200 mark, according to the local chamber of commerce. The city had parks, golf courses, a public library, a residential campus of Colorado Mountain College, and Valley View Hospital. There was a small airport south of the city. The Civilian Conservation Corps built the original runway, and a federal grant made improvements possible in the early 1940s. The Civil Air Patrol has used the facility as a headquarters. Otherwise, operations thus far have been limited to flight training, private craft, and some charter traffic.

The city owns very old rights to Colorado River Basin water. Frank Enzensperger laid the groundwork for the municipal system in 1887 with the start of his project to bring in water from No Name Creek in the west part of the canyon. The system draws water primarily from No Name Creek but can access additional supplies via a tunnel between Grizzly and No Name creeks.

Persons seeking additional insights regarding the city's long history can pursue their areas of interest at the Frontier Historical Museum in Glenwood Springs. In the 32 years since its organization, the Frontier Historical Society has accumulated wide-ranging collections revealing the area's past. The collections are housed in a 1905 residence at 1001 Colorado Avenue. The society received the building in 1971 as a gift from the estate of Mrs. Churchill Shumate, the former Stella Edinger.

IV

CANYON-AREA RAILS

General William Palmer, father of the Denver and Rio Grande Railway Company, envisioned a route through Glenwood Canyon at least six years before Colorado achieved statehood. Rio Grande outlined such a route in its incorporation certificate in 1870. The line, foreseen as a Rio Grande division called Western Colorado Railway, led from Denver to Salt Lake City by way of the canyon. However, about 15 years elapsed before Rio Grande decided to build through the canyon. A number of factors — mining and ranching activity, development of towns, existing Rio Grande routes, engineering considerations, and competition — bore heavily on the decision.

RIO GRANDE SELECTS NEW ROUTE

The then main line of the Denver and Rio Grande reached Gunnison in 1881, going by way of the Royal Gorge, Salida, and Marshall Pass. Construction continued westward to Grand Junction and reached Utah by late 1882.

Denver Public Library Western Collection

Rio Grande rails at one of the Shoshone tunnels, July 23, 1895.

Rio Grande branched from Salida northward to Leadville. It also completed a branch from Gunnison northward to the Crested Butte area, and surveyors in 1881 laid out a right of way leaving this branch at Almont and proceeding up the Taylor River into booming Taylor Park. Rio Grande officials contemplated extension of the proposed Taylor Park line to reach Aspen via Taylor Pass and Ashcroft, and their survey crews soon mapped that stretch also. In addition, they investigated a route to Aspen via Granite. Also under consideration was General Palmer's idea of a route through Glenwood Canyon — from the junction of the Eagle and Colorado rivers, down the Colorado to its confluence with the Roaring Fork River, and onward to Utah — with a branch up the Roaring Fork to Aspen.

The rival Colorado Midland's intentions to build a line to Aspen became public knowledge in 1885. Faced with inroads by Union Pacific and a grade as high as four percent on nearly 80 miles of the Taylor Park route, and seeking a route that was practical for conversion to broad gauge to meet Midland competition and allow handling of traffic from other railroads, Rio Grande decided in 1885 to build through Glenwood Canyon. The grade there was no more than three percent. The route would use existing Rio Grande tracks up the Arkansas River to Salida and north to Leadville. From there it would require new construction — over Tennessee Pass, down the Eagle and Colorado through Glenwood Canyon, and west to Utah.

While Rio Grande worked on this new main line, the standard-gauge Midland tackled construction of its own route — westward from Colorado Springs through South Park to Leadville, through the Continental Divide via the John J. Hagerman Tunnel at Mount Massive, down the Frying Pan River to Basalt, and up the Roaring Fork Valley to Aspen. Both railroads hoped to reach Aspen first and secure lucrative business related to the town's mining boom. In addition, both saw attractive revenue potential in the coal deposits discovered by Walter Devereux south and west of Glenwood Springs. Aspen and Leadville smelters needed coal, and railroads were the only practical means of delivering the large tonnages consumed by smelter furnaces.

Building Through the Canyon

Because the Rio Grande right of way in Glenwood Canyon snaked along the river's south side, a semblance of a burro trail on the opposite bank was of little value to the construction effort. When work on the narrow-gauge grade started in 1886, laborers unloaded equipment and supplies at the terminus of the railroad near the junction of the Eagle and Colorado rivers, loaded them onto wagons, and hauled them to the end of the wagon road at Dotsero. At that point, they transferred the shipments to boats for a hazardous journey down the river to construction camps in the east portion of the canyon. A number of workers drowned.

Laying of ties and rails followed preparation of the rail bed westward and allowed work trains to penetrate the canyon, thereby decreasing the reliance on burros. The earth and rock had to be moved by hand. It was difficult to maintain the necessary work force, and special inducements were required in order to sustain momentum on the most dangerous and difficult jobs. Much blasting was necessary. The project also involved two short tunnels in the Shoshone area as well as the 1,331-foot Jackson Tunnel at the canyon's west end as work progressed to build a ledge for the tracks. Laborers created the necessary width by paring the canyon cliffs and by dumping fill rock into the river channel along the south bank.

Rio Grande's ribbon of rails overcame the canyon's challenges and reached Glenwood Springs on October 5, 1887. Branching up the Roaring Fork Valley, Rio Grande began service to Aspen ahead of the Colorado Midland.

By 1891, Rio Grande completed conversion of its entire main line to broad gauge from Denver to Ogden via the Royal Gorge and Glenwood Canyon. Conversion was relatively easy because of previous installation, prompted by Midland's 1886 arrival in Leadville, of standard-gauge ties from the Leadville area westward to the Colorado River.

Desiring to extend service to Grand Junction, the Colorado Midland was at a disadvantage. With no tracks of its own on

Colorado Department of Transportation

Men and burros work on Rio Grande construction at one of two short
tunnels at Shoshone.

the western part of its planned route, Midland leased the right to use Rio Grande tracks on that stretch.

In 1900, Denver was 289 miles from Glenwood Springs via the Midland and 366 on the Rio Grande.

OTHER INTERESTS EYE CANYON AREA

The Rio Grande and the Midland were not the only companies with visions of tracks between eastern slope cities and Utah by way of the Glenwood Canyon area.

Union Pacific & Western Colorado Railway Company received right-of-way approval through Glenwood Canyon from the U.S. Department of Interior on December 30, 1886. A route change, principally to eliminate a tight curve by running the track in a straight line past a horseshoe bend in the river, received Interior's green light on February 23, 1887. Approval from the Glenwood Springs branch of the U.S. Land Office followed on March 25, "subject to all valid existing rights" of the Greeley, Salt Lake & Pacific Railway Company; Denver & Rio Grande Railway Company; Grand Valley Railway Company; and Colorado Railway Company. Grand Valley Railway Company came into existence as a replacement for a construction arm of the Rio Grande in 1886, while Rio Grande was in receivership. Another early survey showed a route north of the river for the Greeley, Salt Lake, & Pacific Railway.

The planned Union Pacific route was across the river from the Rio Grande, on the north side. It wound eastward from Glenwood Springs through the full length of the canyon, a rail distance of 12.49 miles.

The Chicago, Burlington & Quincy, an affiliate of both the Colorado Midland and the Union Pacific, began work on the grade just east of Glenwood Springs in 1887. O. Meredith Wilson, based on his exhaustive study of Rio Grande documents, wrote that Rio Grande had launched the extension of its line along the Colorado River through Glenwood Canyon "to keep the Union Pacific out." In any case, work on the north bank soon stopped.

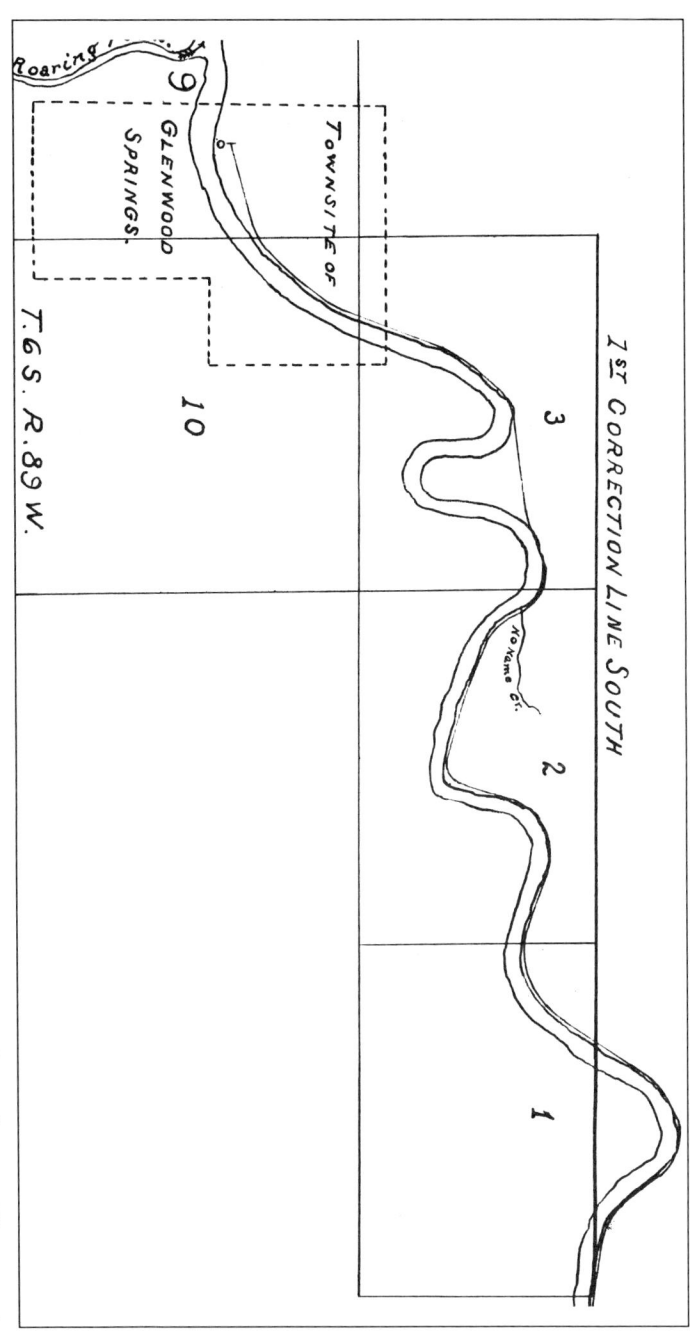

Part of survey diagram — proposed Union Pacific & Western Colorado Railway route. Area shown: Glenwood Springs east through canyon to point within a mile of Grizzly Creek. Shows revision bypassing horseshoe bend just east of Glenwood Springs. Route revision approved, U.S. Department of Interior, February 1887. Right of way is north of river. Rio Grande route is south.

U.S. Land Office Records

In accordance with federal legislation of 1906 and 1909 aimed at recovery of unused right-of-way grants, the General Land Office issued a forfeiture order concerning the Greeley, Salt Lake & Pacific right of way, effective April 5, 1920. Similar action against the Union Pacific & Western Colorado Railway took place on July 12, 1926. Had a railroad been built along either of these rights of way north of the river, Glenwood Canyon might never have seen a highway.

DEATH RIDES RAILS AT DOTSERO

The worst tragedy ever recorded in the Glenwood Canyon area was the 1909 crash of two Rio Grande trains near the west switch of the Dotsero siding, about six miles east of the canyon. According to details distilled from a variety of press reports, westbound passenger train No. 5 and the third section of eastbound freight No. 66 collided on Friday night, January 15.

Before the engineers became aware of the imminent collision and hit the brakes, the passenger train reportedly was traveling 35 miles per hour, while the doubleheader freight had slowed to eight miles per hour in order to enter the siding. So powerful was the head-on crash that it telescoped the three engines into an unrecognizable mass of iron and steel.

Twenty-one men, women, and children died at the scene or prior to reaching medical treatment. A relief train reached the scene on Saturday morning and took the approximately 30 injured persons to the Glenwood Sanitarium for treatment. Five of the injured succumbed later to injuries or complications.

Most of the 26 deaths occurred among occupants of a chair car. The car, made principally of wood and reinforced by metal rods and bars, disintegrated in the crash.

Thomas Cadwallader, a widely traveled officer of Illinois Match Company of Joliet, was in that car but survived. Quoted by a newspaper, he claimed the wreck was his third similar escape from death:

Part of wreckage from 1909 collision of Rio Grande trains at Dotsero.

The first one was in Peoria, Ill., where the entire train back of the smoking car was derailed and toppled over, several being killed. . . . The second one was . . . north of Indianapolis, in which the sleeper I was in turned over twice down an embankment, the rest of the train going through the bridge and burning up. . . .

The *Avalanche*, a Glenwood Springs newspaper, said it contacted freight engineer Sig. Olsen of Glenwood Springs.* In part, his reported account of the tragedy said:

---

* Spelling of the name Olsen, with respect to engineers of both trains, differed from paper to paper and sometimes in successive articles in the same paper. Cemetery records indicated that the correct spelling of the freight engineer's name was *Olsen*. We have used this spelling in all references to him, regardless of the spellings used in source materials. Similarly, and to avoid confusion, all references to the *passenger* engineer have been standardized as *Olson*.

. . . it has always been a habit of mine in making a stop or switch to shut off my power before I got to a stop so as to allow the brakeman to alight without danger to himself who is going to throw the switch. Just on this [the Glenwood Springs] side of Dotsero . . . there is a straight stretch of track and just before you get to the straight stretch there is a curve. Well, we were just in this curve . . . when I saw the reflection of the headlight of the passenger train and thought they were waiting for us at the switch. We went on the straight stretch of track and I had just thrown off my power when I saw the electric headlight ahead of me . . . and then I knew that a collision could not be avoided. . . . I blew the whistle to warn Jeffries on the back engine, threw on the emergency brake, jumped over the firebox door, which the fireman had left open and then jumped in the air. . . . before I hit the ground the crash came.

I rolled down the bank with machinery rolling on top of me. . . . hot water from the engine began to wash out in my face and on my body. . . . the water washed dirt and stuff on me until nothing but my head was clear.

Sig. Olsen's fireman John Anderson found him but needed the help of two other men to free him from the debris.

According to the *Avalanche*, Olsen said he had worked with the engineer of the passenger train. He said, " 'I fired for Gus for over two years before I got an engine of my own. . . . I have always found him to be a very careful and cautious man and would rather run against him than any other man on the road.' "

Eagle County Coroner J. G. Gilpin held an inquest in Redcliff on January 23. The coroner's jury reached a conclusion that the cause of the wreck was passenger engineer Gustave Olson of Grand Junction " 'disobeying orders through negligence or some unknown cause.' "

Conductor Al McCurdy testified that Olson whistled as the

eastbound passenger train neared the west switch at the Dotsero siding at 9:46. According to a newspaper report of his testimony, "Brakeman [F. J.] Roberts was on the platform and called through the door of the smoker where McCurdy was seated and reported No. 66 not there." McCurdy "then gave a signal to Olson to stop at once." Olson hit the brakes hard, slowing the passenger train to 20 to 25 miles per hour before impact.

A newspaper said the testimony of head brakeman F. J. Roberts supported that of McCurdy:

> After reaching the siding and noticing that Olson ran right through he thought possibly the order might have read to wait at Dotsero until 9:45, he said, as it was then that time instead of 9:55 as he understood the order.
>
> He at once asked Conductor McCurdy about it, he said, telling him the freight was not there and McCurdy then gave the signal to stop.
>
> The witness . . . said in his opinion [the wreck] was caused by Olson misreading his watch or else that Olson had been confused by the reversed directions for meeting the two sections of the freight train given in the train order delivered to him at Wolcott.

Dispatcher C. D. Wightman, who issued the orders for the trains to meet at Dotsero, repeated the orders from memory. District Attorney James T. Hogan had a copy of the order issued to the passenger train. Said the *Avalanche:*

> It directed that train to wait for the third section of No. 66, the freight, at Dotsero, until 9:55, and to pass second section 66 at Gypsum.
>
> The passenger train would reach Gypsum before Dotsero and Wightman explained he reversed the order of passing because the second portion, relating to second section of No. 66, was issued subsequently to enable that train to get to Gypsum instead of waiting at Dotsero with the third section.

There was testimony that the ground was covered by snow, but track conditions were good.

In the aftermath of the collision, Glenwood citizens helped in many ways. Ladies volunteered as nurses, caring for the injured at the sanitarium and delivering flowers and prayers to each room. The men helped notify next of kin, assisted Rio Grande personnel in arranging transportation and communications for survivors and their relatives, and helped with shipment of the deceased. In a letter printed by a Glenwood Springs newspaper, survivor Thomas Cadwallader lavished praise upon the people of Glenwood for their " 'loving attention, kindness, and sympathy.' "

MOFFAT ROAD DESTINED
TO BENEFIT RIO GRANDE

Denver banker David H. Moffat, a former Rio Grande president, organized the Denver, Northwestern & Pacific railroad project in 1902. His plans included the capture of the transportation business along a route between Denver and Salt Lake City. Moffat's 1911 death and a lack of funds forced the company to scale down its plans and reorganize as the Denver & Salt Lake Railroad, often called *The Moffat Road*. The Moffat Road built track from Denver westward over Rollins Pass to Granby, Hot Sulphur Springs, Steamboat Springs, and Craig.

The Moffat won a victory in 1922 when the Colorado General Assembly approved formation of the Moffat Tunnel Improvement District. Upon completion in early 1928, the six-mile tunnel, with its east portal a few miles west of Rollinsville and the west portal at Winter Park, enabled Moffat trains to negotiate the Continental Divide without the expensive snow-related problems and steep grades associated with Rollins Pass.

With track completed only as far as Craig, the Moffat was unable to compete for the important Denver to Salt Lake business. And revenue sources along its 230-mile route were few and poorly diversified. The Moffat existed almost entirely on shipments of coal and products from farms and ranches.

The Moffat's troubles greatly benefitted Rio Grande. Officials negotiated an agreement that allowed Rio Grande trains to use Moffat tracks through the tunnel. Further, near the beginning of 1935, Rio Grande completed the Dotsero Cutoff, linking its main line with that of the Moffat where the two routes were only 35 miles apart. The cutoff ran from Dotsero, just northeast of Glenwood Canyon, northward to a place called Orestod — Dotsero spelled backwards — near Bond. By using the Dotsero Cutoff and the Moffat Tunnel, Rio Grande slashed 175 miles from its run between Glenwood Springs and Denver. The distance by way of the Royal Gorge was 360 miles but only 185 via the Dotsero Cutoff and Moffat Tunnel. In April 1947, Rio Grande acquired all the assets of the ill-fated Moffat Road.

The very small settlement of Dotsero was named for an Indian chief's daughter. Settlers began using the name no later than 1883. In May of that year, James L. Riland mentioned Dotsero in an account of activity in the area. We don't know whether settlers pronounced the name as Dot-sair'-oh or Dot-seer'-oh. But railroaders apparently perpetuated the third pronunciation Dot-zero' that many people use today. According to Rio Grande literature, surveyors gave rise to this usage when in 1885 they began work at this spot and marked their starting point on a map with a dot and a zero.*

MIDLAND SCRAPPED

The Hagerman Tunnel failed to overcome weather-related problems in connection with Midland's crossing of the Continental Divide. Crews had great difficulty keeping the approaches cleared of snow. Train accidents and delays were frequent there. A related firm bored another tunnel, known as Busk-Ivanhoe, below the Hagerman.

---

* Sources for the name's origin include: Dawson, *Place Names in Colorado*, 18; Wolle, *Stampede to Timberline*, 261; & "Vista-Dome Views," a California Zephyr promotion pamphlet, 6.

Detroit Publishing Company   Colorado Historical Society 25148

View toward west from railroad grade circa 1900. Today, I-70 Reverse
Curve Tunnel passes through cliff at right, near mile mark 127.

Both Rio Grande and Midland still showed economic scars
inflicted by the loss of silver-ore shipments following the silver
panic of the 1890s. Hopes for the Midland evaporated when the
Federal Government selected Rio Grande as the carrier for personnel and supplies during World War I. Midland fell victim to
its lifelong unprofitability during the war. Its last train ran

through Busk-Ivanhoe in summer 1918, the road became scrap, and the Rio Grande no longer faced competition in the Glenwood Springs area. However, Rio Grande itself was in serious trouble.

RIO GRANDE STUNG BY WAR, COURT

The Rio Grande railbed and equipment deteriorated during World War I, and a "Slow Order" went into effect for all trains between Glenwood Springs and Minturn. Maximum allowable speed for freight trains was 15 miles per hour. But poor condition of locomotives sometimes imposed its own limits, preventing trains from attaining that speed.

Rail tycoon Jay Gould invested heavily in Rio Grande stock in the late 1800s and controlled the company for a time. Rio Grande helped finance Gould's construction of the Western Pacific between Utah and California, completed in 1910. Court action developed in connection with Western Pacific financing. In 1917, the U.S. Supreme Court unleashed a bombshell, a decision that plunged Rio Grande into receivership early in the following year. Because Rio Grande helped finance Western Pacific, the high court held Rio Grande liable for payment of both principal and interest on Western Pacific bonds. The ruling resulted in the demise of the Denver & Rio Grande Railroad Company on July 31, 1921. There was a reorganization, and the old Rio Grande emerged from receivership as the Denver & Rio Grande *Western*.

Laurene Grant Knupp of Eagle, Colorado was among Rio Grande passengers in the 1920s:

We often went to Glenwood on the train, because we had four trains a day, two each way. So you could go down in the morning and come back in the evening.

RIO GRANDE WESTERN MODERNIZES

Denver & Rio Grande Western, Western Pacific, and Burlington launched a cooperative venture that became the pride of the rails. The sleek, silver-colored California Zephyr began its runs between Chicago and Oakland on March 21, 1949. It was the

Frontier Historical Museum, Glenwood Springs, Colorado

The California Zephyr in Glenwood Canyon.

nation's first transcontinental streamliner, and it was destined to outlive all of its privately operated brethren. The Zephyr, with its revolutionary Vista-Dome coaches, offered a measure of luxury the airlines have yet to approach. The dining car featured five chefs, fine tableware, and Colorado carnations. The train had plenty of room for passengers to walk, socialize, and view the countryside.

Seats on the second floors of the glass-roofed Vista-Domes were not reserved. That allowed passengers to come and go as they pleased. The air-conditioned Vista-Domes featured wall-to-wall carpet, reclining seats, restrooms, public address systems, and music from radios and wire recordings.* Completing the air of luxury inside the stainless steel coaches were murals, rear luggage compartments as well as overhead storage, venetian blinds, and hostesses called Zephyrettes. For sleeping-car passengers, there was a Vista-Dome observation lounge providing valet service, buffet, magazine library, writing desk, and a shower-equipped drawing room.

Rio Grande kept its system in good repair and exhibited a progressive stance in its operations. The late Gilbert A. Lathrop, a railroader and writer on railroad subjects, called the Rio Grande of the 1950s "one of the most modern . . . Class A lines" in the nation. According to Lathrop, the rails were made of 112-pound to 136-pound steel, and the ties were chemically treated to discourage insects and rot.** These were stabilized by a bed of slag ballast. Safety was enhanced by modification of curves to decrease their severity and by a centralized traffic-control system for the block signals.

PETRAFESO RECALLS LONG CAREER

Louis Petrafeso began his career with the Rio Grande at Grand Junction "right out of high school," when he was 19. In a

---

* Recordings made on spools of steel wire preceded the perfection of magnetic tape.
** A yard length of rail weighed 112 to 136 pounds.

1993 interview with your author, Petrafeso said that, except for a
period of military service, he worked on Rio Grande from 1942 to
1985. He worked initially as a fireman, feeding the coal-hungry
locomotives during their thunderous journeys through Glenwood Canyon. Some of his trips ran along the Colorado River
between Grand Junction and Bond, and some were from Grand
Junction, up the Colorado to the Eagle River, and up the Eagle to
Minturn. Bond and Minturn both were crew-change locations.
Petrafeso said, "We used to laugh about Dotsero being the biggest
Y in the United States. One leg of it went to Denver from Dotsero,
and the other leg went to Pueblo." The fireman's job was a big
and important one. "The fireman was the wheel in them days,"
he said. "That was kind of a funny feeling, because you knew that
if you didn't keep it hot and keep the steam up, the train would-
n't get to the other end of the road." When diesels replaced steam
engines, "it made you feel kinda' unimportant," he added.

He ran steam locomotives, "traded off with the engineer,"
but "never made a pay trip on the road with a *steam* engine, as
an engineer." He was in line for promotion to engineer on the
Rio Grande when the Army drafted him for overseas service in a
railroad battalion during World War II. "So I was runnin' steam
engines over the jungle of India. When we went to the service,
they promoted all of us. I was promoted and had a regular job as
an engineer over there in India before I was 21 years old," he
said. Upon his return to the Rio Grande after serving in the
Army, he found that the steam engines were "just about gone."

Petrafeso remembered rocks and deer as frequent problems
in Glenwood Canyon:

> I guess the biggest problem you had was rocks. It
> was quite a hill . . . going eastbound from Grizzly to
> Shoshone. That was our hardest pull, up through there.
> As the years went by, they kept putting more and more
> slide fences in there.

Deer were especially troublesome in the canyon, said Petrafeso,
and the Grizzly Creek area was a particularly bad stretch:

Deer always crossed the track there. The track was between the river and the hill. They'd come down and get their noses in that water, and you'd come around a curve, especially at night, and there was no way to prevent hittin' 'em. We hit more deer and elk in the Glenwood Canyon than on any other part of the division.

The trains never got Joe Madalone's goat. Madalone, section foreman at Shoshone, had a billy goat that spent considerable time in a railroad tunnel across the river from the section house. Louis Petrafeso recalled, "We'd catch that ol' goat oftentimes in that tunnel, and that wise ol' guy would just lean against the side of that tunnel, and nobody ever hit 'im."

Petrafeso told of an experience aboard a diesel engine passing through Shoshone following a snowslide. Railroad crews had completed a cut through the slide, and:

We was comin' through there on a train, comin' down fairly slow, and I see Joe standing on the snow that was about even with the cab. I opened the window and honked the horn and waved, and he was standin' there, leanin' on his shovel. About the time I got there, that son of a gun threw a big scoop of snow right in the engine, hit me in the face. I didn't open the window for him anymore.

Joe was quite a character. He raised a family there.

ALLEN TAKES A NOSTALGIC LOOK

Fred R. Allen was with the Civilian Conservation Corps in 1934, when his camp moved to the J. E. Sayre property that was used later as an internment site for Nazi prisoners of World War II and eventually was given to Glenwood Springs for a city park. Another relocation of the CCC camp around 1938 took Allen to Colorado National Monument, and it was in nearby Grand Junction that he met Norma, his wife to be.

Fred R. Allen photo   Fred R. Allen collection

Westbound on Rio Grande at Shoshone, 1970s. Block signal is red.
U.S. 6 & 24 and old bridge visible, center right.

In our 1994 interview, Allen said he went to work for the Rio
Grande in 1942 at Grand Junction and stayed with the road for
41 years as a fireman and engineer. Most of his runs were
through Glenwood Canyon to Bond or Minturn. Bond was the
halfway point between Grand Junction and Denver. Minturn,
near present Vail, was the midpoint between Grand Junction and
Pueblo.

Allen experienced the transition from steam-powered locomotives to those powered by diesel engines. As a fireman, he
often shoveled 30 tons of coal into the firebox on the run between
Grand Junction and Minturn or Bond. He said that most of the
big steam engines had stokers, augers that moved the coal up
into "the pot." "You never knew until you got called whether it
was going to be a hand-fired engine or what," he said.

Fred R. Allen photo   Fred R. Allen collection

The reason for the red signal:
section of slide fence broken.

Rail operations for the Glenwood vicinity centered on Funston, just across the river from the west part of Glenwood
Springs. Fred's wife Norma recalled, "They had a beanery there;
while the trains were being watered and refilled with coal, the
engineer and fireman would usually get a little snack." The
beanery and the old freight station were eliminated in a late
1960s renovation of the Funston yards.

Asked his opinion of the biggest difference between steam
locomotives and diesels, Fred Allen laughed and said, "The
physical labor involved." He added that the most important
advantage of diesels was their superior efficiency. And diesels
were more efficient to maintain. Generally, all they needed was
diesel in their fuel tanks and sand in their sand boxes, and they
were ready to roll. Diesels were more predictable, allowing the

performance of many maintenance operations at planned intervals. In contrast, steam locomotives had to go into the roundhouse for maintenance after every run.

Most of the road's early diesel acquisitions were EMDs, manufactured by the Electromotive Division of General Motors. Early diesels on the Rio Grande came also from ALCO, the American Locomotive Company. The California Zephyr used three ALCO diesel units.

The railroad experimented with a small number of diesel-hydraulic locomotives from Germany. The locomotive technology on Rio Grande was mainly the diesel-*electric* type, in which a diesel engine drove an electric generator that in turn powered traction motors, one on each axle. But the German diesel-*hydraulic* was direct drive, the wheels receiving their power through U joints directly from the diesel engine. "They weren't successful," recalled Allen, explaining that "they did just fine in lower and flat country, but they couldn't get enough air in tunnels and high altitude," so the railroad sold them.

Allen received a promotion to engineer in 1955, the year in which diesels sidelined the last of the steam engines on his runs. He pointed out that it was yet a number of years before he had a regular job as an engineer. There was no set time, he said. "It all depended on how business was, and you bounced back and forth as the youngest engineer or the oldest fireman," based on seniority. For "quite a few years," the diesels carried a full crew. There'd be "engineer, fireman, and head-end brakeman on the head end of the train and the conductor and a rear brakeman on the rear."

Fred recalled spring and winter as the worst times of year in Glenwood Canyon. In spring, "It would thaw in the day, then freeze at night; water would get in cracks in the rocks, freeze and expand, and you'd get a lot of rock slides."

Allen spoke of a 1968 wreck of the eastbound California Zephyr in the canyon. Rounding a curve near Shoshone on March 29, engineer William R. Farmer of Grand Junction saw rocks on the track immediately ahead. Farmer activated the emergency brake, but the lead diesel unit derailed, and Farmer rode it over a 35-foot embankment and into the river. Fortunately, he escaped injury and remained conscious, because he landed with his head in the water with " 'my feet sticking up in the air, and everything in the cab was on top of me,' " according to a quote in the *Rocky Mountain News*. As a second diesel unit and a steam generator followed the lead diesel over the embankment, fireman Dan C. Raff of Grand Junction jumped. He escaped serious injury.

Two additional diesel sections, three coaches, a baggage car, and a diner also left the track but stopped short of the embankment. There were no injuries among the 189 passengers on the train.

The wreck affected not only eastbound passengers but those on the westbound Zephyr, which waited on the track at Dotsero. After a series of maneuvers lasting about eight hours, passengers from both trains were back on the road to their destinations. According to the *Rocky Mountain News* article, Rio Grande pulled eastbound passengers back to Glenwood Springs aboard coaches unaffected by the wreck, then took them from Glenwood to Dotsero by bus. They turned the waiting westbound Zephyr around, and it became the eastbound. Meantime, westbound passengers went by bus from Dotsero to Glenwood Springs, where undamaged coaches from the wreck became the westbound Zephyr.

Fred Allen said that railroaders faced the hazards of snowslides in winter. "When there was a big snowslide, you'd wonder if there were any rocks in it, or was it all snow. But you'd hit it and hope."

Summer also had its drawbacks, especially for a fireman. During Allen's coal-firing days, 16 hours was the maximum allowable length of shift, and "16 hours in one of those steam engines was a long time," he said. Trains often failed to reach their crew-change locations before the 16-hour deadline passed. In those cases, the railroad called in "doggin' crews" to bring the trains in.

Railroad wrecks in the canyon were not nearly as common as those on the highway. Fred Allen's wife Norma said that Fred saw cars in the river on several occasions and asked the crew to radio for help.

Some results of California Zephyr derailment west of Shoshone,
March 1968.

Fred R. Allen photos   Fred R. Allen collection

Summing up the railroad days, Norma Allen said, "As a wife, I was very honored and very proud of what Freddy had done" with his life and career.

PASSENGER ERA FADES

In the 1950s, long-haul trucks cut into the freight business, travelers demonstrated a preference for automobiles, and the government shifted mail contracts and other subsidies in favor of the airlines. It was the beginning of the end for the great passenger era on the railroads.

In 1969, Rio Grande rail operations became part of Rio Grande Industries, Inc. During the following 15 years, this holding company also operated businesses unrelated to transportation, including real estate development, computer timeshare facilities, and manufacture of rides for amusement parks.

Glenwood Gets Last Look at Original Zephyr

It was March 1970. The Burlington and the Western Pacific had decided to terminate operation of the California Zephyr on their two-thirds of the route, and the Interstate Commerce Commission had approved discontinuance. The Zephyr already had made its last westbound journey, and the final eastbound trip from Oakland to Chicago was underway when engineer Fred R. Allen boarded the sleek train for the segment from Grand Junction through Glenwood Canyon to Bond. Allen discovered that the system of scheduling had placed an unusual combination of crew members in the cab:

At that time, I was on the Engineers Extra Board, and I was the youngest man on there. The fellow that followed me in seniority was the oldest fireman in seniority. I got out running and [found out] he was my fireman. I was the youngest engineer, and he was the oldest fireman.

Fred R. Allen collection

Westbound Rio Grande freight at Grizzly Creek. Engineer Fred Allen captured view from cab of his eastbound train in the 1970s.

Allen recalled the fireman's name as Clare Trinklein. "That was the end of the original California Zephyr, run by the Burlington and the Rio Grande and the Western Pacific," he said. After ending their part of the trip at Bond, the two deadheaded back to Grand Junction on a freight.

AMTRAK BYPASSES CANYON AT FIRST

Amtrak, a government-backed venture to preserve the nation's passenger service, began operation in 1971. Amtrak inaugurated a California Zephyr of its own and incorporated some of the original Zephyr's rolling stock. But Amtrak chose Union Pacific tracks across Wyoming rather than the Rio Grande route through Colorado.

Rio Grande filled part of the void with its *Rio Grande* Zephyr between Denver and Salt Lake. Running westbound on Mondays, Thursdays, and Saturdays, and traveling eastbound on Tuesdays, Fridays, and Sundays, there were generally nine cars — Vista-Domes and traditional coaches, a club car, and dining car. Basic one-way, adult fare on the full trip was $70.75 in August 1982. Scheduled travel time between Glenwood Springs and Denver was some five hours and twenty minutes. Rio Grande was posting a three-million-dollar annual loss on the train's operation between Salt Lake and Denver.

With almost all of its revenues arising from freight — mostly coal, lumber, steel, autos and auto parts, and food products — Rio Grande in April 1983 terminated its Zephyr and became strictly a freight line. The discontinuance marked the end of the great passenger era that fostered the development of the American West and opened the way for later transitions from wagons to autos and from trains to jet aircraft.

Engineer on the last Grand Junction to Denver run of the Rio Grande (Denver) Zephyr was John Schoening, a veteran of the rails who was near retirement.

Working From Steam to Diesel, Rio Grande to Amtrak

In 43 years on the rails, John Schoening of Grand Junction saw service on both freight and passenger trains and on both the Rio Grande and Amtrak. In a 1993 interview, he recalled rail operations in the Glenwood area.

Schoening started with Rio Grande as a fireman in May 1942 and fired freight locomotives between Grand Junction and Minturn or Bond. He received a promotion to engineer in 1951 but had no regular job as an engineer until the mid 1960s. "Nineteen sixty six was about the first time that I started running an engine on my own," he said.

Conrad F. Schader

Part of a D & RGW freight, Glenwood Canyon, October 1976.

He said that Mallets provided Rio Grande's power in the later years of steam locomotives. The majority of engines on freights were Mallet 1500s, 1600s, and 3600s. Passenger trains used mostly Mallets of the 1700 and 1800 series. The road had some 1200s in passenger service and as helpers, and there were still some hand-fired 1100s in use. The last steam power on the system thundered along the rails in the mid 1950s.

Schoening spent about two years, beginning in 1966, as an engineer out of Glenwood Springs on the Aspen Branch:

> We hauled the lumber and stuff up into Aspen, and we went to Woody Creek, and we picked up . . . about 10 cars of ore [about] twice a week. . . . Then we picked up

the coal at Mid-Continent down at Carbondale . . .
around 40 cars. . . . We'd take that and our ore and go to
Glenwood and set it out in the Funston yards.

Mainline freights picked up the ore and coal cars at Funston and
hauled them to industrial customers such as Geneva Steel, Kaiser
Aluminum at Fontana, California, and Colorado Fuel and Iron in
Pueblo.

Amtrak Switches to Canyon Route

In July 1983, Amtrak abandoned the Wyoming route and
switched its California Zephyr onto Rio Grande tracks for the
segment between Denver and Salt Lake City, restoring transcontinental passenger service through Glenwood Canyon. The
Zephyr soon became Amtrak's most popular train.
    One of Amtrak's engineers between Grand Junction and
Denver was John Schoening:

> I worked two years on Amtrak out of Grand Junction.
> . . . James Church was the senior man . . . on Amtrak out
> of here. . . . We had two jobs out of here — Jimmy and
> myself.
>   We would work over to Denver, back to Grand Junc-
> tion, and then we had two days off, and then we would
> go again. Whenever I had two days off, Jimmy would
> work. . . . Jimmy became ill and couldn't work anymore,
> and Louis Petrafeso took over Jimmy's turn.

RIO GRANDE SOLD AND SOLD AGAIN

Deregulation and a number of mergers among western railroads hurt the smaller roads and prompted Rio Grande Industries to focus more closely on its basic business. In early 1983, Rio
Grande implemented a cooperative operations and marketing

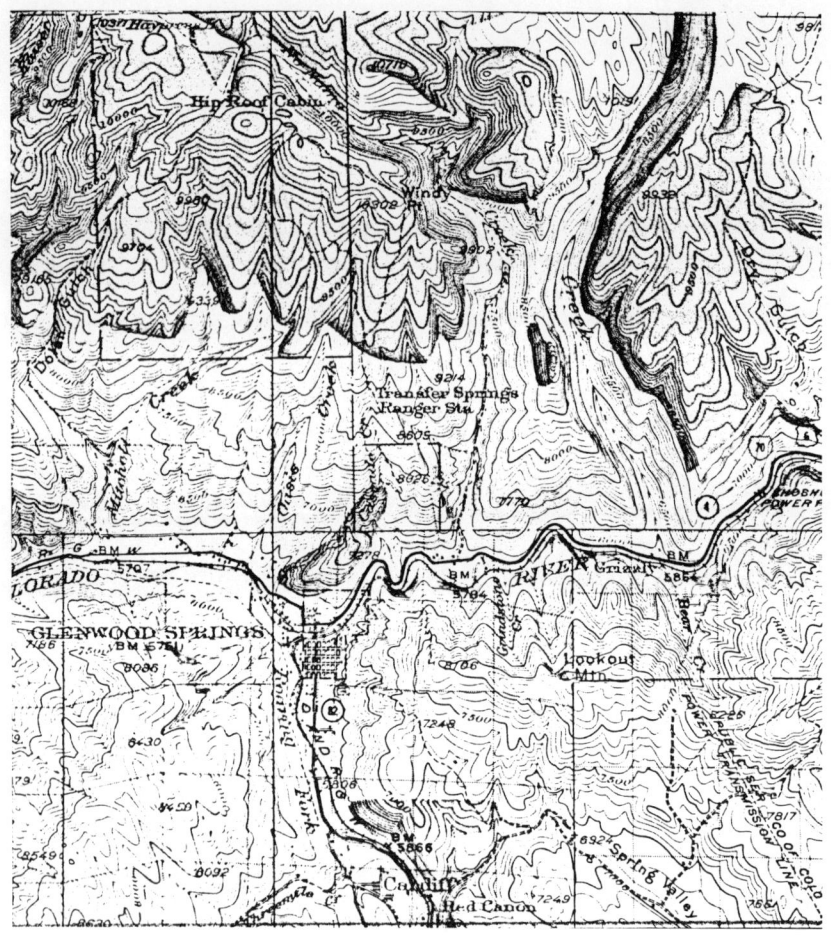

U.S. Geological Survey map

This page and following page:
Glenwood Canyon and vicinity.
Portion of Glenwood Springs Quadrangle, 1927,
partial revision of 1962.
Blocks and streets of Glenwood Springs
are at lower left.
At far right, careful observation
reveals some detail of the Dotsero Siding.

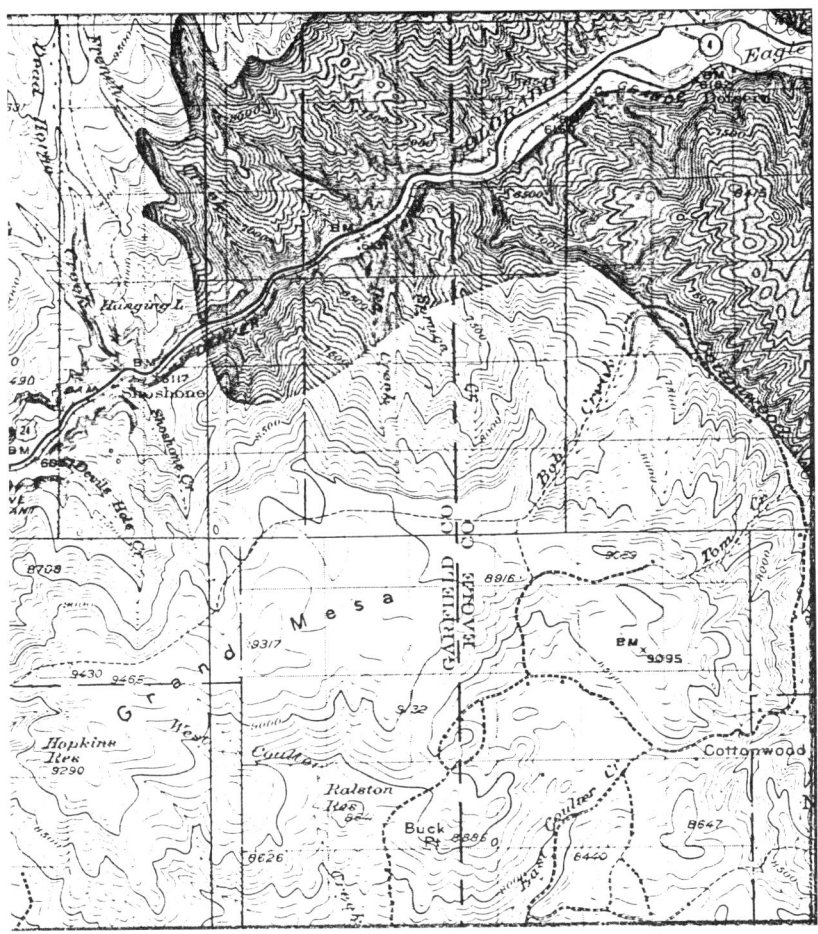

U.S. Archives and Records Administration

agreement with the Southern Pacific and in the next year began talks with companies viewed as potential buyers of the Rio Grande Railroad. The talks culminated in the 1984 sale of the Rio Grande to Denver billionaire Philip F. Anschutz. Four years later, Anschutz bought the Southern Pacific and combined it with the Rio Grande. According to Norma Allen, there was no scarcity of tears among Rio Grande railroaders and their families when Southern Pacific logos began to replace those of Rio Grande, and the Southern Pacific red and gray began to cover the familiar black and orange of the Rio Grande on the locomotives.

Philip Anschutz in 1995 opened yet another chapter in the history of the Glenwood Canyon rails. Anschutz in August completed an arrangement to sell the Southern Pacific Rail Corporation to Union Pacific. Some people saw irony in the 5.4-billion-dollar proposal. If approved by regulatory agencies and the stockholders of both corporations, the merger would deliver Rio Grande, which in the 1880s had discouraged Union Pacific efforts to build through Glenwood Canyon, into the hands of Union Pacific.

V

MORE SETTLEMENTS AND THE NATIONAL FOREST

Small settlements — mostly farm and ranch efforts — emerged rapidly in the 1880s wherever there was space for a home and a few cows or fruit trees. A small number of more substantial settlements grew later on the roots of old homesteads, and the reasons for their evolution included tourism, expanded farming and ranching, railroad and highway operations, and the generation of electric power.

SILOAM SPRINGS

Siloam Springs was a resort project that failed to reach its potential. The site at the east end of Glenwood Canyon embraced both banks of the Colorado River and an intervening island.

C. A. McBrairty, Fred A. Metcalf, and George Rust filed a plat of the proposed development when they founded the

Siloam Springs Sanitation and Town Company around the beginning of 1884. The men hoped to attract affluent business people, and their plans were correspondingly impressive. Plans included a hotel, hot-springs bathing facilities, train station, and even a hospital, situated along a grid of wide streets.

Much of the planned development materialized, including a bath house, train station, and a hotel and some houses built of logs. Before the Rio Grande Railroad reached Glenwood Springs, Siloam was a popular resort. The settlement experienced boom conditions when it was briefly the terminus of the Rio Grande while track construction advanced westward through the canyon. After Rio Grande reached Glenwood Springs in 1887, Glenwood's rapidly developing facilities lured visitors away from Siloam.

Ranchers purchased some of Siloam's buildings and relocated them. Tom Baxter bought the early hotel and moved it a short distance east to Dotsero. The townsite became part of what is now the Bair Ranch. J. Golden Bair's wife Thelma said the hotel building apparently became the main residence on the ranch. She said the arrangement and sizes of the rooms in the ranch house were consistent with those of an old hotel. On the townsite itself, the only remaining evidence of Siloam Springs in the early 1990s consisted of some concrete blocks that apparently had been the foundation of a building.

BAIR RANCH

Because of its improbable rescue from the brink of early failure and its eventual size and longevity, the Bair Ranch holds a prominent place in Glenwood Canyon history. The story of this development spans more than 75 years of operation by members of the Bair family and their associates. It is a story of hard work, the once volatile relationship between cattlemen and sheepmen, a love of the outdoors, skillful management of finances, and the knowledge, creativity, and determination to deal with a variety of problems.

Bair Ranch had a shaky beginning at the east end of Glenwood Canyon in 1919 when sheepman Joseph E. Bair formed a partnership with George Mayne and George Dunsdon. Mayne, Bair, and Dunsdon mortgaged their farms at Alpine, Utah and acquired the Allen Cattle Ranch in Glenwood Canyon. They purchased mules, a camp outfit, and 1,800 sheep.

Members of the cattlemen's associations quickly learned of the ranch purchase and warned the fledgling partnership of serious consequences in the event of any attempt to move sheep onto the ranch.

In spring 1920, the company sent the sheep to Glenwood Canyon by train. Knowing that cattlemen would be waiting at the Dotsero stockyards, the sheepmen decided to unload at Shoshone, about three miles west of Dotsero and deep within the canyon, despite a lack of corrals and feed there.

The sheep arrived at the Shoshone siding in the teeth of a rain and snow onslaught that lasted three days. And it took all three days to herd the recently sheared animals onto the south ledges of the canyon where there was forage. The sheep became cold and wet, and 400 of them never made it beyond the Rio Grande right of way. Some 200 had died previously on winter range in Utah, so the original herd of 1,800 had dwindled to 1,200.

Faced with these losses and the mortgages on their Utah properties, the partners were in serious trouble. George Dunsdon and Joseph Bair left to seek employment, but George Mayne stayed. Mayne enlisted the aid of Joseph Bair's 21-year-old son Elmer in an effort to salvage the venture. Joseph promised Elmer a 50 percent interest in his share of the operation if the ranch could be saved.

Mayne and Bair struggled to build and maintain lines of credit to finance ranch operations. Each year brought a new crop of lambs. Each year, some of the sheep went to market, providing income and making possible the control and retirement of debt. The range was good, and the sheep found ample water in Ike Creek and a number of lesser streams. The ranch became a success.

When business conditions improved, Joseph Bair and George Dunsdon came back, said Elmer in a 1993 interview. After four or five years, the partners "split up among themselves; Mayne sold out to Dad, and finally he bought Dunsdon out," he said.

Elmer Bair and Ida Lorena Smith were married on the ranch in October 1921. Elmer ferried the guests across the river in a small boat.

Each year, the sheep were sent to the Utah desert for the winter. They were shipped at least as far as Mack, Colorado and from there were trailed into the desert.

When it was necessary to herd the sheep to and from the summer range north of the river, there were two choices — trail them more than six miles upstream to the bridge at Gypsum or swim them across the river near the ranch. The latter was a dangerous job made more difficult by the animals' dislike of water. Under low water conditions, it was possible to cross the river on horseback. Even then, the horses waded in water up to their bellies.

Diversions were few, especially in winter when it was not only necessary to ford the river but to negotiate the snow-clogged canyon road. On occasion, the Bairs visited friends down the canyon by hitching a ride with section workers on a railroad handcar.

The ranchers received welcome help from crew members of the local trains. When Rio Grande engineers spied passengers on the tracks, they picked them up and took them to town. Train crews also dropped off mail and groceries that had been delivered to the Glenwood Springs depot. Residents repaid their benefactors with lamb and other products of the ranch.

In early 1923, Elmer helped build a footbridge across the Colorado at Dotsero. It somewhat eased access to the Bair and Baxter-Anderson ranches.

Elmer arranged to withdraw his interest in the Mayne, Bair, and Dunsdon partnership in 1925, and he and his family embarked on a two-and-a-half-day auto trip to Alpine, Utah.

W. T. Lee photo   U.S. Geological Survey 2928

Westbound along Pikes Peak Ocean to Ocean Highway, east end of
canyon, 1925. Rangelands of Bair Ranch lie to south on relatively level
terrain behind canyon rim.

But in 1926, they came back to Colorado, and Elmer went to
work for the Yule Marble Company at the community of Marble, southeast of Glenwood Springs. He served four years on
the town council and for a time as a town marshal. In the 1929-
1930 winter, traveling on skis, he worked as a private carrier of
mail between Marble and a mine at the headwaters of the Crystal River on Schofield Pass.

However, Elmer's future and the realization of his boyhood dreams lay not in those endeavors but in ranching, and in 1931 he and former trapper Lew Vibrans became partners in the livestock business. They started with 200 sheep and options on homesteaded lands on Cottonwood Mesa, above the old Mayne, Bair, and Dunsdon ranch.

While the two worked to establish their ranch, cattlemen harassed them. For example, cattlemen several times herded cattle into the midst of the ewes and lambs. And, said Elmer in his autobiography, they started a range fire in an apparent effort to burn the sheep.

The Bair-Vibrans partnership ended with the accidental death of Lew Vibrans. Elmer Bair purchased Lew's interest in the ranch and proceeded to build the large operation he had envisioned in early childhood.

As neighboring properties became available, Elmer purchased them. Attached to some of those acquisitions were grazing leases for federal lands, which further extended the ranch's carrying capacity. The line between Eagle and Garfield counties was approximately in the middle of the ranch. In the early 1930s, two of Elmer's brothers, J. Golden and Howard, homesteaded on lands adjacent to the ranch.

Elmer Wins Landmark Case

Congressional passage of the Taylor Grazing Act in the 1930s resulted in designation of certain federal lands as grazing areas for cattle only. If a sheep rancher owned land behind a designated cattle area, he had the right to cross the cattle range as long as he traveled three miles per day in doing so. After crossing some of this land a number of times with sheep, Elmer was each time arrested on trespassing complaints:

I was hauled in there and tried in Justice of the Peace Court three or four times. When I was convicted in them J. P. Courts, I was put under five-thousand-dollar bonds. At that time, 'twas a dollar as big as a cartwheel. They were sure that I couldn't pay that, but those boys there in Gypsum [Summerfield and Thomas] that'd been run out by the cowboys . . . went my bonds each time.

Elmer's lawyer was Bill Noonan of Glenwood Springs:

He's the guy that finally got shot there. He was one of the best range lawyers in the country. The first two or three times they took me over there and tried me in J. P. Court, Noonan was busy in lawsuits, and he couldn't be there, so he got a lawyer up at Eagle, and he changed the court to a greater court. We went from one to the other 'til it was a test case for the whole country.

In the test case, the cattlemen wanted to use a straight-line measurement to determine whether the three-mile-per-day requirement had been met. But Elmer and lawyer Bill Noonan contended that the proper method of measurement was not as the crow flies but as sheep walk — up hills and down hills and around obstacles. The landmark case, first trial in the new Eagle County Courthouse, ended with a decision in Elmer Bair's favor despite the jury composition of eleven cowmen and only one sheepman.

Brush With Death Marks Turning Point

By 1940, Elmer ran 5,500 adult sheep and 150 cattle. The operation encompassed more than 11,000 acres, some owned by the ranch and some leased from the Federal Government and such private interests as the mining company at Marble.

Elmer and his wife Ida moved to Carbondale in 1939. Early the next decade, Elmer contracted two serious illnesses simultaneously, and doctors believed his death was imminent. But Elmer survived, resolving to decrease his business involvement and become more active in the Mormon Church.

Ordained as an elder, he helped establish a Sunday school in Glenwood Springs. He became president of the Glenwood Springs branch upon its establishment in the 1940s, oversaw construction and 1949 completion of the church's own building in the city, became president of the Western Colorado District, and in 1955 rose to the position of patriarch.

In 1960, Elmer disposed of his sheep outfit. However, he and his wife remained associated with ranching for five more summers by operating a spread near Burns, Colorado for Texas builder and Baptist minister Ray Williamson.

Elmer, in our 1993 interview, reminisced about the old Allen Ranch — the start of the Mayne-Bair-Dunsdon operation in Glenwood Canyon:

> This man [Charley] Allen was a bachelor, I imagine in his 30s when we came. He had [an unmarried] sister we didn't see, but she lived there on the place with him until the time we came.
>
> In the spring, when it was thawing out, rocks used to come down. . . . This one time, a rock had come down on Flynn's Curve about a mile east of the Allen Ranch. The train hit it that night and throwed the engine off the track, killed the engineer. His name was Flynn. The fireman caught a tie; it was really in the high water. . . . In the middle of the night, this fireman caught the tie and was goin' past the ranch ahollerin' for help. Allen's sister ran out . . . and grabbed a boat and caught him and saved him from drowning. The railroad put in a spur there, so they could load cattle and unload there on the place. . . . That was how [the Allen Spur] came to be put there.

Bair said that the original owner of the ranch, before the Allens took over, was Ike Barrier, a bachelor and bear hunter at the time. Barrier's early presence there gave rise to the name Ike Creek, the main drainage through the ranch. The creek enters the Colorado River from the south near Mile Mark 129. Recalled Bair:

The first government trapper . . . stayed with Ike quite a little. Then he came and trapped with us for a while on his first assignment and told me quite a lotta stories about Ike and the country then.

Bair said that the trapper told him that Barrier had settled there in the 1880s:

It was while they was buildin' the railroad down the country . . . he, with Barrier and others, hunted meat for the railroad people.

Elmer Bair's memories included the beauty of Glenwood Canyon and the Flat Tops and the satisfaction of achieving his boyhood dreams. He was thankful for a partnership of more than 73 years with his wife Ida. He wrote of appreciation for most of the wildlife and the fishing that was "too good" on the Flat Tops. But not all the memories were pleasant. He wrote of crows pecking the eyes of sheep trapped to their shoulders in snow, the bloody wool of dead and injured sheep in the wake of attacks by the extremely adaptable coyotes, and eagles harassing wild, bighorn sheep, forcing the lambs into plunges from canyon cliffs, and swooping to catch the animals as they tumbled from ledge to ledge.

Ida Bair died January 22, 1995 in Glenwood Springs. She was 95.

At the time of this writing, Elmer's brother James Golden Bair and wife Thelma lived on the old Mayne-Bair-Dunsdon Ranch in Glenwood Canyon, Golden's home for some 73 years. "My father brought me out here when I was 12 years old, and I just stayed here," said Golden. "My boys [Craig and LeGrande] run the ranch now," he added.

The ranch continued primarily as a sheep operation and spanned some 6,000 acres in 1993. "We have run cows, but we didn't have any luck with 'em, so we just stay with the sheep," he said in a 1993 interview. Those sheep numbered about 5,000 then, and they continued to fall prey to coyotes. Golden said,

"Coyotes killed a lamb . . . right in front of my son's camper that he's got here. My grandson was out shootin' baskets [and the coyote] was so close that my grandson got scared and went inside."

Bair Ranch Rest Area just off Interstate 70 was once part of this ranch. The Bairs gave up some land for the rest area in exchange for improved access to their property. The interstate construction included a bridge across the river for the Bairs' vehicles. Just when the new span neared completion in 1984, high water washed away the old footbridge.

HANGING LAKE PARK AND RESORT

The Hanging Lake resort consisted of a restaurant, accommodations for a few tourists, a gasoline station, and the Hanging Lake Trailhead. Situated on the north side of the highway, the resort's best years were the 1920s and 1930s. It became a stop for early cross-country motorists and enjoyed popularity among canyon-area residents as a destination for pleasure drives.

The City of Glenwood Springs bought the 1.5-acre lake and about 760 adjacent acres from the government in 1924 as a municipal park. The Civilian Conservation Corps improved an old trail to the 25-foot-deep lake in the 1930s.

Visitors had their choice of walking to the lake or renting burros for easier negotiation of the one-mile trail. Steep in places, the trail climbed through the north wall of Glenwood Canyon by way of a side canyon along Dead Horse Creek. The trail led to a natural, spring-fed lake idyllically perched in a cliff ledge some 2,000 feet above the Colorado River.

With the number of hikers eventually running as high as 50,000 per year, the trail ranked among Colorado's most popular. Glenwood Springs returned the lake to the Federal Government in the early 1970s, and the trailhead resort gave way later to I-70 construction. Hanging Lake remains accessible, but the trailhead now sits along the recreation path about 0.5 mile east of the Hanging Lake Rest Area.

Conrad F. Schader
Partial view of Hanging Lake, June 1977.

HYDRO PROJECT SPARKS DEVELOPMENT AT SHOSHONE

Shoshone, near the canyon's midpoint, was the site of early ranch activity, a couple of Rio Grande section houses, a siding, and a water tank for the steam locomotives. Its biggest days came during construction of Shoshone Dam and the related hydroelectric plant. Activity on the canyon floor centered on three locations — a construction camp, the dam, and the power plant — a couple of miles apart.

Upstream from the site of the dam, apparently at a place used in earlier days by Rio Grande construction crews near

This page and next: Main headquarters and camp,
Central Colorado Power Company, circa 1910.

Colorado Historical Society 25149

Colorado Historical Society 25143

Looking upstream at little community at Shoshone Power Plant.
Left of river: canyon highway, living and office quarters.
Rio Grande railbed on opposite bank. Date unknown.

Cinnamon Creek, Central Colorado Power Company established a camp to serve as a headquarters for the company and
to provide food, shelter, and medical attention for a workforce
that eventually rose to 1,000 men. In addition to the diversion
dam and power plant, the ambitious project included a tunnel

to carry water from the dam to the downstream power plant and a rail station and river bridge at the camp.

The three-million-dollar undertaking began in December 1906. Preliminary work included installation of a temporary water-driven generator to supply some of the energy for construction.

A U.S. post office opened in the camp in 1907. Its name was Shoshone, and the official date of its establishment was September 3.

The concrete dam was 20 feet high and 245 feet long. Its location was the head of Shoshone Falls, also called Cottonwood Falls. A large tent erected over the site allowed work to continue during cold weather.

The name of the railroad siding at the construction camp was Shoshone. Rio Grande had another siding, named Higby, across the river from the power plant. The siding received its name in recognition of a Colonel Higby, a consultant on construction of the water tunnel. Colonel Higby died at the work site when a derrick cable parted and dropped the hoist's load on him. Five persons lost their lives in other accidents during construction of the Shoshone facilities.

Power generation started in June 1909 on a test basis, and full production began in the following month. In the final system, water diverted at the dam flowed into the concrete-lined tunnel 12 feet high and 16 feet in width and raced westward through the canyon's north wall to the power plant 2.7 miles away.

The power plant contained two 9,000-horsepower, horizontal turbines, each fed by a penstock nine feet in diameter and giving the water a fall of 287 feet. Each turbine ran at 400 revolutions per minute and drove a 7.2-megawatt, 4,000-volt alternating-current generator. While the two generators gave the plant a production rating of 14.4 megawatts, output of 16 megawatts reportedly was possible during periods of high flow in the river.

As a result of decreased demand for its services following the departure of construction workers, operation of the

M. R. Campbell photo   U.S. Geological Survey 1140A

Shoshone plant, Colorado Power Company, 1915.

Shoshone Post Office ended in 1910. Official date of discontinuance was June 30.

Following a foreclosure, Colorado Power Company, a Central Colorado Power Company successor, took control of the Shoshone plant in 1913. Two years later, a 115,000-volt transmission line was completed a distance of some 160 miles and across three passes on the Continental Divide — Hagerman, Fremont, and Argentine — to deliver electricity to Denver.

Public Service Company of Colorado, then part of a utility empire controlled by Henry Doherty, acquired the installation through a September 1924 merger with Colorado Power Company. At that time, in addition to supplying some of Denver's electricity, Shoshone served Leadville, Salida, and most of the San Luis Valley.

Alice M. Koonce of Eagle, in a 1996 interview, said her father John D. Randall worked for Public Service Company at Shoshone from approximately 1926 into the 1950s, and "we lived in the canyon for many years." When he went to work there:

> He had a degree in engineering from Colorado University. He was chief engineer. Once a year, they shut all the turbines down and cleaned them up, worked them over. He was in charge of all of that. And if anything went wrong, he was [essentially] in charge. Later on, he was superintendent.

For a number of years, the company provided living quarters at the plant for employees engaged in operation and maintenance. Alice Koonce recalled:

> There were five families living there and a boarding house which housed the single fellows. It was a definite little community, because at that time the road to town was a very narrow, almost one-way, dirt road. It was a great place to live, actually.
>
> There were four houses — two single-story houses next to the river, and up on the hill fairly close to the power plant, west of it, was a two-story house which had two apartments in it. The boarding house was just east of the plant. It was a two-story building with one small apartment upstairs, and downstairs were the housekeeper and the cook, rooms for the single guys, a room with a pool table, and so forth. At the dam, there

W. T. Lee photo   U.S. Geological Survey 2916

Shoshone Dam from below, 1925.

also was a house, but the caretaker of the dam was the only one who lived there.

Widening of the highway displaced these buildings in the 1930s. The company relocated them downstream just west of Grizzly Creek.

Public Service Company of Colorado became an independent, autonomous corporation in the early 1940s. Shoshone in

1995 remained among the company's production facilities, operated around the clock, and employed about 15 full-time workers.

GRIZZLY CREEK SCENE INSPIRES RAILCAR DESIGN

A small settlement developed on the north side of the canyon near the confluence of Grizzly Creek and the Colorado River. The creek received its name from the well-publicized shooting of an exceptionally large bear by George P. Ryan in 1881. Ryan was a prospector, hunter, rancher, and early Garfield County Commissioner who had come to Colorado in search of adventure.

The creek descends rapidly through a side canyon that remains wild. This canyon narrows to an impenetrable jungle of rock and vegetation as one follows a fading trail upward along the stream.

Early homesteaders planted orchards just north of the river at Grizzly. People who lived in the area in the 1920s remembered a man named Brackney and many a trip to his orchards for sweet cherries, apples, and other fruit. Retired rancher Elmer Bair noted that wild bighorn sheep often visited Brackney and exhibited no fear of him:

But they'd stand a way back when we'd go there to visit. He could get away from us, and they'd come right up and eat [apples] out of his hand.

The scenery at Grizzly Gulch inspired the design of a two-story, glass-domed railcar that gave passengers a full view of the surrounding countryside. C. R. Osborn, a General Motors Vice President who managed the Electromotive Division, envisioned the revolutionary design while riding a Rio Grande train at Grizzly on July 4, 1944. From Osborn's idea, General Motors designers developed a ten-foot model and sent it to the

Schutte Collection

Frontier Historical Museum,
Glenwood Springs, Colorado

Burlington shops, where a remodeled Burlington coach became the first Vista-Dome railcar. This prototype made its debut in Glenwood Canyon in July 1945 during a Chicago to San Francisco run of the Exposition Flyer, a 1939 predecessor of the California Zephyr.

In tribute to this design concept, Rio Grande, in cooperation with Garfield County and the highway department, placed the Vista-Dome model atop a stone monument near Grizzly on a pulloff beside U.S. Highways 6 and 24 in September 1950. But the monument became a target for vandals. To preserve the model, road foreman Gene Harden removed it from the monument and placed it in the Glenwood Springs depot. The model later found a home in the Colorado Railroad Museum at Golden.

Grizzly Creek was also the meeting place of the California Zephyrs during the years they ran both eastbound and westbound on a daily basis.

Around 1975, the Grizzly Creek settlement included two gasoline stations, a park for recreational vehicles, two sets of cabins, and at least one nearby home. About 20 people lived at Grizzly in 1980. Colorado needed the land for Interstate 70, and all but two of the residents moved out by the end of September 1981.

One of explanatory plaques on Vista-Dome Monument at Grizzly Creek.

Conrad F. Schader

The final, private owner of a gas station at Grizzly was the John White family. Blue Sky Adventures, a raft business operated by Chuck Lanci, rented land and buildings from the Whites for three years. When the Whites moved away in 1981 after their property came under state ownership, the raft firm rented its quarters from the state for the 1981 season and carried between 50 and 100 rafters down the river each day. Another firm, Rocky Mountain Rafting, operated just upstream from Lanci and also leased land from the state for a time. The leases expired at the end of September, forcing both companies to vacate their canyon quarters.

Downstream, between Grizzly Creek and No Name, a highway maintenance shop and a couple of residences stood for many years, the location a memorable one because of the lush, neatly kept lawns complementing a towering pair of beautifully symmetrical spruce trees. Said Alice Koonce:

> Those were the houses that had originally been up there at Shoshone Plant. Public Service Company no longer wanted to be involved in real estate like that, so they sold it to my father [no later than the mid 1940s]. My parents lived in one [of the residences]. They rented the other house.

When Interstate 70 displaced the maintenance facility and residences, contractors spared the two spruces. However, the apparent condition of these monarchs in 1993 indicated a losing battle for survival.

WHAT'S IN THE NAME OF NO NAME?

When they first hear the name or catch a glimpse of it on the Exit 119 sign along I-70, many first-time visitors are surprised, curious, and unbelieving. The name is *No Name*, and it identifies an I-70 rest area near the west end of the canyon, an adjacent settlement, and a creek.

The community received its name from No Name Creek. Len Shoemaker said that he received instructions, while working as a ranger for the U.S. Forest Service around 1919, to assign names to some geographic features that had no official names. Shoemaker wrote in one of his books that No Name Creek was among them. However, the name was apparently in use, at least locally, in the 1800s. It appeared on the map of a survey showing the proposed route for the Union Pacific & Western Colorado Railway.

A one-word form of the name has been seen in some later reference materials. On the 1887 diagram, a two-word form was used.*

In a 1993 interview, longtime resident Elwyn Schrock said the community took its name from the creek. "It's strictly from the creek," he said.

Homesteaders established the roots of the community in the early 1880s. They constructed a number of buildings and conducted ranch and farm operations that included the planting of apple orchards. H. T. Sale homesteaded on Cascade Creek. J. C. Brown and Rush Pratt chose the canyon of No Name Creek and called their homestead Cobblehurst, and the locations of their houses appeared on an 1880s survey diagram.

No Name obviously made a favorable impression on Buster Gardner, a member of the cast in a Tom Mix movie that was filmed in the canyon in 1926. He joined C. R. McCarthy in construction of some tourist cabins along the creek.

Ida Pratt once had a snack shop on the former Sale homestead. Nearby, Blanche Brown operated a resort called Hide-a-Way. The resort's dance pavilion made it a popular entertainment spot.

A flume that carried water along the north face of the canyon to Glenwood Springs overflowed, forming a little stream that crossed the road and wound its way down to the river just below No Name. The ground near that junction was

_____

* U.S. Archives, Denver.

an ideal picnic spot, according to area residents who enjoyed it around 1930. The site reportedly gave way to the residence of a Glenwood Springs theatre owner. The residence in turn yielded to later highway improvements.

When the Schrocks moved to No Name in 1961, they discovered that winter weather froze the line that fed No Name Creek water to the community. Other homes had cisterns that assured a supply in the colder months, but the Schrock residence lacked such a backup source. A friend who operated a concrete-mixer truck brought water to help the Schrocks through that first winter. Schrock soon built his own cistern. In addition, he and a friend tried to keep the line open from the creek. He said, "I remember going up and knocking the ice off that intake at two and three o'clock in the morning. Then they voted to put in a whole new water line, dig it down so it wouldn't freeze. I kind of engineered that one."

Schrock served about 12 years as president of the No Name Water Association and was a member of the board for approximately 5 additional years. He spoke of the mid 1960s, when the first I-70 construction took place at the west edge of the canyon: "We tried to get the highway department to build us a whole new line there, but they wouldn't do that. But they did build us a new intake and some filters that we put in our water line."

The settlement saw some growth within the past 30 years, some of the changes attributed to Schrock himself. Performing the tasks with his own hands, he constructed three homes and remodeled five others. Schrock said he foresaw little potential for future growth because of a scarcity of suitable building sites. "We're just about saturated according to county planning," he explained.

In 1993, No Name consisted of approximately 60 homes clustered at the lower end of No Name Creek near the junction with the Colorado River and strung out upstream along the creek, mobile home and RV parks, and the I-70 No Name Rest Area. Population was about 150, excluding residents of the mobile home park.

Conrad F. Schader

River floaters east of No Name, August 1985. Upstream view with railroad grade at right. I-70 construction, center BG above U.S. 6.

Schrock, a school teacher for 30 years in Glenwood Springs, noted that "there were a lot of apple orchards out here at one time, and there was a lot of irrigation. When the highway came through, they cut off all the irrigation that went to the old No Name." The short segment of highway between No Name and Glenwood Springs was the first four-lane segment within the canyon. This section opened in 1965 and included twin tunnels to eliminate the bothersome curve where U.S. 6 and 24 followed a horseshoe bend in the river.

Construction of I-70 and the rest area reclaimed an old gravel pit at No Name. Near the canyon rim to the north, a one-time limestone quarry remained inactive.

Employees of Shoshone Power Plant and Colorado Department of Transportation and residents of Bair Ranch and the No Name community were the only people allowed to remain in the canyon full time after completion of I-70.

NATION'S SECOND FOREST ADJOINS CANYON

President Benjamin Harrison signed a proclamation establishing the nation's second forest reserve — White River Timber Land Reserve — in October 1891.* The reserve sprawled across the White River Plateau from Glenwood Canyon northward to the White River and from McCoy westward to Meeker.

It was a veritable fairyland of abundant natural resources. There were large stands of evergreens punctuated by grassy park-like expanses, lakes, and flat-topped peaks. Elk, deer, mountain sheep, bear, and a host of smaller animals inhabited the area, often called the Flat Tops.

The large size of the reserve stunned even the staunchest conservationists. It brought new life to opposition that had erupted upon rumors of the planned designation. In Glenwood Springs and other communities, there were fears that the reserve would stifle development, but subsequent efforts to decrease the size of the reserve failed because of poor support from the general public. Denver businessmen favored the reserve. Even at that early time, Denver thirsted for the forest's water to help sustain development.

The government had transferred ownership of various parcels of land to other interests prior to formation of the reserve. These lands — mainly homesteads, patented mining claims, and townsites — were allowed to remain in private hands when the reserve was created.

The excellent plateau habitat that once assured the Utes a plentiful supply of game continued to provide good populations of animals for later hunters. President Theodore Roosevelt's trips to the White River Reserve publicized the plateau's wide range of resources in the early 1900s, and the region became a favorite with hunters of big game.

Roosevelt hunted on the plateau twice during his 1901 to 1909 presidency. While the presidential visits were ostensibly

---

* Yellowstone was the first.

pleasure trips, they gave Roosevelt the opportunity to meet local people and convince some opponents to join him in support of the White River Reserve and efforts to establish a highly controversial permit system to control grazing.

Roosevelt's hunting trip of spring 1905 was particularly important. It came as the Forest Service moved into a pivotal reorganization guided by Gifford Pinchot and supported by Roosevelt. According to a biography of William R. Kreutzer, the nation's first forest ranger, the reorganization resulted in such actions as removal of requirements for political endorsements from the selection process for rangers. More importantly, it set the course of the Forest Service toward the higher ideals of the forestry profession and solidified the multiple-use concept that still underlies management of the national forests.

Park Designation Proposed

Controversy flared anew upon word of a Federal Government proposal, reportedly backed by Roosevelt, to designate the White River Reserve as a national park. Management policies for parks were stricter than those for forests, and opponents said a national park would seriously damage the economic health of the area by inflicting hardships on miners, loggers, and ranchers. Proponents argued that a park designation was appropriate and would attract tourists. Because of local opposition and significant opposition among legislators, the government abandoned the park idea.

Congressional action in 1907 changed the name of White River *Forest Reserve* to White River *National Forest*. The legislation applied the same type of name alteration to the other forest reserves in the United States.

The Holy Cross Forest, designated in 1905, later became part of the White River Forest. That merger added vast areas south and east of Glenwood Canyon to White River, raising its total expanse to more than 1,198,000 acres.

Canyon Area Offers Recreation Opportunities

The recreation path through Glenwood Canyon provides an avenue for those who wish to gain a closer relationship with the canyon and some of the lands that lie within White River National Forest. This hiking and biking corridor and the connecting trails provide access to the canyon for fishing, photography, and a leisurely look at the rock strata, the tall evergreens tenaciously surviving on meagre soils of the cliff ledges, and the innovative design of Interstate 70.

Many fishing opportunities lie along the river. Some of the tributary streams also support gamefish but are difficult to fish because of brush and steep slopes.

In 1995, the river within the canyon contained brown and rainbow trout, some whitefish near the west end, and rough fish such as suckers. Effective at least for the five years beginning with 1996, state wildlife officials decreased the trout limit from eight to two on a long stretch of the Colorado, including the Glenwood Canyon section. The Roaring Fork River, which joins the Colorado from the south in Glenwood Springs, is one of the most famous fisheries in the state. Special regulations apply there.

Additional fishing spots are found at small lakes on the plateau north of Glenwood Canyon. A number of these are accessible by way of trails and wagon roads. Maps and information on locations, status, and accessibility are available from the White River National Forest office in Glenwood Springs. Stores that specialize in sporting goods are additional sources of information.

VI

EARLY TRAILS, ROADS, HIGHWAYS

The Utes had no complete trail through Glenwood Canyon. And more than a decade after completion of the Denver & Rio Grande track, there was still no continuous wagon road through the canyon. However, the canyon was destined to become a major thoroughfare not just for trains but for horses and wagons, autos, trucks, and buses.

EARLY ROUTES BYPASS CANYON

The first trails in the Glenwood area resulted from repeated use of certain routes by animals seeking food and water and migrating between summer and winter habitats. Thousands of years ago, ancestors of the Utes used many of those same trails and for the same reasons. Because the cliffs extended right down into the river in most of Glenwood Canyon, human travel through the full length of the chasm was impossible except at times of unusually low water. However, the Utes and their ancestors gained access to parts of the canyon via trails near both ends and through side canyons cut by the river's tributary creeks.

Supply avenues to the Glenwood Springs area in the early 1880s were tortuous trails used by pack-burro trains and horses. Improvement of some stretches of these paths, parts of which were old Ute trails, made them passable for horse-drawn wagons, sleighs, and stagecoaches, provided the routes were sufficiently free of snowdrifts and mud. There were early pack trails and wagon roads both north and south of Glenwood Canyon. On some segments, the road builders collected tolls.

An 1888 map of Garfield County showed a trail, known as the Carbonate Trail, leaving the north bank of the Colorado near the east end of Glenwood Canyon at Dotsero, climbing the White River Plateau, and running westward to Carbonate. Extensions of this trail came into Glenwood Springs from the north. One followed Canyon Creek to the Glenwood vicinity. Another led from Carbonate to Windy Point and Transfer Springs. From there, two branches headed south, one following a fairly direct line to the west side of Glenwood Springs, the other descending roughly along Cascade Creek to the east side of town. Improvement of the trails between Windy Point and Glenwood allowed the passage of stagecoaches in 1883. For a number of years, stages used these roads in transporting tourists across the Flat Tops to Deep, Marvine, and Trappers lakes.

An important path came into Glenwood Springs from the south via Schofield Pass. The route went from Gunnison northward to the East River, up the river to Crested Butte and Gothic, over Schofield Pass, and down the Crystal River drainage to the Colorado.

Glenwood Springs was accessible also from a number of pack trails that converged on Aspen from the east and south. These paths shared a common route from Aspen to Glenwood by way of the Roaring Fork Valley. Three routes, first as pack trails and later as rough roads for stages and wagons headed primarily for Aspen, ran west from the Arkansas Valley. One was the Independence Trail west from Twin Lakes and over Independence Pass. Many traffic jams occurred on that route in 1882. Another went west from Buena Vista, over 12,126-foot Cottonwood Pass, across Taylor Park and Taylor Pass, and down to Aspen. The third, known as the Virginia, Hillerton, and Roaring Fork Toll Road, left the Arkansas south of Buena Vista and reached Aspen by way of Tin Cup Pass, Taylor Park, and Taylor Pass. There was another route from Taylor Park to Ashcroft and Aspen via Pearl Pass.

Yet another access developed. It left the Colorado at Gypsum and ran south of Glenwood Canyon across Cottonwood Mesa and 8,280-foot Cottonwood Pass, not to be confused with the Cottonwood Pass mentioned earlier. Several branches descended from the mesa to the Roaring Fork Valley. Settlers began construction of the first wagon road linking Aspen and Glenwood Springs in late 1882 and completed it about two years later. The early routes were not dependable. Deep snows often blocked the passes from late summer into spring. Even in mid summer, rains and melting snows sometimes created muddy quagmires and delayed traffic.

The Rio Grande's arrival in Glenwood Springs in 1887 freed the town from its dependence on unpredictable trails and wagon roads. However, the old roads were still important to outlying settlements that had no rails, and some of the old routes remained in use well into the 20th century. As many of the little settlements faded, most of the old roads fell into disuse and deteriorated. In the 1950s, some of these became popular with off-road enthusiasts. Some remain in use today for ranch operations and recreational travel on foot, on horseback, or in vehicles designed for off-road travel. The road over Independence Pass between Twin Lakes and Glenwood Springs via Aspen became State Highway 82, although the pass itself had no pavement until the 1970s.

In Glenwood Canyon itself, there was a poorly defined burro route situated roughly along the unimproved railroad right of way on the river's north bank. Surveyors, freighters, and homesteaders gradually picked away at it, and by the late 1890s the tortuous route became sporadically passable for wagons. There were steep places to negotiate and a number of streams to ford. Worse yet, the path lacked continuity.

TAYLOR CHAMPIONS CANYON ROUTE

State Senator Edward T. Taylor of Glenwood Springs convinced the Colorado General Assembly in 1899 to approve a measure funding construction of a wagon road from Denver to Grand Junction and permitting the use of convict labor on the project. Stipulations accompanied the legislature's approval, including preservation of natural beauty where possible and a prohibition of roadside advertisements.

The project included the first, coordinated effort to build a road the entire length of Glenwood Canyon. Blasting crews had to cut back the towering cliffs in order to make room for the road. Because so many cliff faces extended all the way down into the river, the only way the crews could reach their work areas was to approach the sheer cliffs from above with ropes and rope ladders. That was one of the reasons the canyon work was so costly. The canyon segment accounted for half of the $60,000 total cost of the road. Completion of the route, called the Taylor State Road in honor of Senator Taylor, came in 1902.

W. W. Price of Colorado Springs piloted a Winton along Taylor State Road through Glenwood Canyon in 1902.

Road racer Barney Oldfield negotiated the nerve-wracking stretch by automobile during a transcontinental competition in 1906. The race established a number of records for auto travel.

The Colorado General Assembly in spring 1909 established a highway commission to direct construction of a system of state road. State Senator Edward T. Taylor was instrumental in achieving passage of the legislation.

In 1910, 13-year-old Morgan Gavin steered a Thomas Flyer from Carbondale to Cincinnati by way of the canyon, Colorado Springs, and Denver. Two years later, Gavin and two companions

Colorado Department of Transportation

Westbound on Taylor State Road.

Colorado Historical Society 25147

Looking west, Glenwood Canyon. Probably during upgrade to
Pikes Peak Ocean to Ocean Highway.
Rio Grande roadbed visible, lower center, to left of river.

braved the canyon, pushed onward to Tennessee Pass and Leadville, crossed South Park to Colorado Springs, and continued to Denver.

The early expeditions behind the wheel, especially the widely publicized Oldfield journey, popularized auto travel, created public support for road building, and led to designation of certain routes as national thoroughfares. The allure of auto travel attracted the adventurous to America's fledgling network of roads, and an increasing number of pioneer motorists undertook long trips. From these roots grew America's enduring love affair with the automobile.

People of the Glenwood area responded enthusiastically when vehicles powered by electricity, steam, and gasoline became available. But Glenwood was by no means alone, and strong competition developed among Western Slope towns vying for inclusion in coast-to-coast auto routes.

Canyon Included on U.S. Routes

In 1912, the route traveled by Morgan Gavin and his companions received recognition as part of the Lincoln Transcontinental Highway. Two years later, the highway through Glenwood Canyon received the designation as part of the Pikes Peak Ocean to Ocean Highway. There were no bridges. For stream crossings, the highway dipped through fords — places where the creek banks had been scooped out to allow vehicles to drive across the creek beds. Some of these received cement pavement.

Former schoolteacher Laurene Grant Knupp of Eagle, Colorado said of the Pikes Peak Ocean to Ocean Highway:

It was scary. It was for me, anyway. But I was just a kid. One time, we went to Glenwood to the circus. My Dad had a Model T. . . . We left [Eagle] before daylight. We'd have flat tires, and my Dad would have to patch them. We got to Glenwood in time for the two o'clock circus.

Auto is eastbound at the "Half Tunnel" east of French Creek.

The road would be rough and corrugated in spots. I especially remember between here and Gypsum — how awfully rough it was, and how slick it would get when it rained.

Retired rancher Elmer Bair said the highway was still a wagon road when he came to the canyon in 1920, "never been a grader of any kind, never been no work on it, and the only time you could get through with a wagon was in summer." In winter, canyon-area residents sometimes attempted the trip using teams and sleighs.

For one man at least, the poor condition of the road provided a good source of income. Said Bair:

In the spring, early, when the runoff came . . . the water'd get on the [railroad] track down by the Allen Ranch, and it got on the old wagon road. A fellow, Al Sweet from Dotsero, moved down there with a pair of mules. There was a few of them old Fords just startin' to get on the road. And he'd pull 'em through that water and charge 'em five dollars a trip. You could hear old Al hollerin' at them mules any time of the night. It was straight across from the ranch.

PIKES PEAK HIGHWAY UPGRADED

The U.S. Surveyor General's office in Denver approved the route of the Pikes Peak Ocean to Ocean Highway on August 30, 1921. Colorado and Garfield County put as many as 400 convicts from the state penitentiary at Cañon City to work in the canyon in 1923. The men started at the Glenwood Springs end and worked eastward for two summers to build the highway's first graded and graveled surface.

Doctor Recalls Highway

Doctor Woodrow E. Brown, a retired medical doctor living at the Colorado town of Hotchkiss, grew up in Eagle and rode

Colorado Historical Society 25146

Downstream view, 1931. Pikes Peak Ocean to Ocean Highway
at right, railroad at left. Cliff at left is today the
site of Hanging Lake Tunnels.

the canyon highway, "many, many times in the late 1920s in a 1923 Chevrolet touring car. He said, "The road was extremely narrow," total width about 1.5 lanes, "and if you met a car, you darn sure got over, got a wide place, and let 'em go by." Below Shoshone Dam, there was a big cliff; the road wound around it in a turn of some 180 degrees:

> It was a pretty good dropoff into the canyon there. Then the road got fairly steep, and we went down quite a grade there. I remember in springtime the river used to get really high and just boil down through there. The spray off of that rapid, right below the dam, used to travel clear up onto the road.

That area of the canyon was a perennial trouble spot. The churning water at Shoshone Falls, later known as Cottonwood Falls, undermined the highway and chewed away at the railroad bed on the other side of the river. This place was a big problem in winter, too. It was one of the worst snowslide locations in the canyon.

Mix Movie Filmed in Canyon

The Shoshone Dam vicinity was one of the locations used in the 1926 filming of the western movie *The K & A Train Robbery* starring Tom Mix and Dorothy Dawn. Mix at the time was one of Hollywood's highest-paid actors. Doctor Woodrow Brown, then a lad about eight years of age, recalled:

> We went down there . . . and they stopped us before we went around that sharp curve. When we got out and walked around there so we could see what was going on, here came Tom Mix up the road on his horse Tony, ridin' real hard. . . . He sweeps this girl out [of a buggy] into his arms and comes to a stop just ahead of the place where we were standing. . . . This girl [turned out to be]

Film crew for The K & A Train Robbery at work in the canyon, 1926.

a man dressed up as a woman.* I just thought it was ter-
rible that they would do a thing like that.

Filming continued at a number of locations in the canyon.
In a scene at the east portal of the Jackson railroad tunnel, Tom
Mix:

> . . . was hanging over the track by his hands, and he was
> going to drop onto this train. The train didn't come . . .
> and pretty soon he got so tired that he couldn't hold on
> any longer, and he let go. He dropped down and broke
> his ankle on the railroad track. Later on, maybe a month

---

* A stuntman.

or so, they had a big rodeo in Glenwood Springs, and Tom Mix was the star attraction. We went down to that, and Tom Mix was still in a cast.

Assistants threw tin cans into the air, and the actor pulled his revolver and shot holes in them. "That was the only thing he did that day," said Brown. In recognition of their hospitality, Mix offered Glenwood Springs residents a prizefight and other entertainment events during that year.

CANYON HIGHWAY REBUILT

The canyon highway remained undependable and narrow until the federal and local governments began construction programs to provide jobs during the Great Depression of the 1930s. Thelma Bair, who came to the area in 1937, recalled that the highway was still narrow and unpaved then, although it at least had a gravel surface.

Edward T. Taylor, who had become a member of the U.S. House of Representatives, obtained federal funds for construction of U.S. 6 and 24 in Colorado. The grant included 1.5-million dollars for widening and paving the Glenwood Canyon portion.

Under pressure from labor groups, the Federal Government by that time had taken steps to discourage the use of convict labor on projects that received federal assistance. Making use of Work Projects Administration labor, construction began in 1936. Design engineer was L. L. Finley, while H. L. Jenness served as construction engineer.

Crews blasted more rock from the canyon cliffs and pushed debris into the river to make room for the broader highway. "While they were making this two-lane road . . . we had to go up over Cottonwood Pass to go to town," said Thelma Bair in an interview. East of the canyon, the pass road branched south across the river, climbed Cottonwood Mesa, turned west to cross the mesa, and descended along Cattle Creek to the Roaring Fork Valley.

Motorists brave canyon snow; year unknown.

The full length of improvements for U.S. 6 and 24 in Colorado opened officially on August 1, 1938. The reconstructed highway provided a paved lane eastbound and another westbound for traffic in the canyon.

Grand Junction resident Ruth (Mrs. Cecil) Bowhay, the former

Ruth Brown, grew up in Eagle. She shared memories of the Pikes Peak Ocean to Ocean Highway and its 1930s successor. She said, "It was quite an elation to go over [the new highway] because it was really a doozy before. We didn't have any heat

Eastbound on Pikes Peak Ocean to Ocean Highway, Glenwood Canyon, circa 1930.

George L. Beam photo   Colorado Historical Society 25141

in the car, and we always took bricks and hot-water bottles with us to keep warm." Her childhood memories included the mineral vapors from the hot springs. She explained that you could smell the vapors "quite a ways up from Glenwood, and my brother and I would always have a race to see who could smell them first."

Eastbound auto on horseshoe bend just below No Name,
probably during 1930s improvements for U.S. 6 & 24.

P. J. Kirwin photo

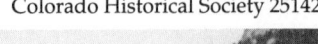
Colorado Historical Society 25142

FORMER SHERIFF REMEMBERS HAPPENINGS

Having served for more than 20 years as sheriff of Garfield County, he was in a good position to observe many of the occurrences along U.S. 6 and 24 in Glenwood Canyon. Ralph Baker, who took office in January 1953, detailed some of his recollections in a 1993 interview.

Over the years, traffic accidents and resultant drownings led the list as causes of death in the gorge. In his 22 years in office, the former sheriff said 84 drownings occurred in the county, most of them in the Colorado River:

Not a big majority, but a majority of them, happened in Glenwood Canyon. We'd get our boats out and go up and grapple. Sometimes we were fortunate enough to hook onto them, and sometimes we had to wait for mother nature to form enough tissue gas for them to float, and then we'd get them out. But out of the 84 drownings, we found 82 of them.

It was carelessness most of the time, cars going in the river. It was strictly a two-lane highway, and that's probably one of the reasons why people went off the road, a lot of it in the shade, and icy spots. They were going too fast going around a curve and got to skidding around there and went off.

One time, we had three boys ride down the river; some people said they went over the dam. One boy disappeared, and we never did find his body. He was one of the two that we didn't find.

Experience taught Baker some things about removal of autos from the Colorado:

They'll always be headed upstream, due to the fact that the gas tank is on the back, and it's usually about half full, or maybe less than that, but there's a certain amount of buoyancy there. Your motor is in the front, and it's

Above: Anglers try their luck where water from Shoshone Power Plant returns to river. September 1979.
Below: Idyllic-appearing picnic spot on river's north bank, east part of canyon near Tie Gulch, October 1976.

Conrad F. Schader photos

heavy, and it goes down first and naturally will turn around and head upstream. When we grappled for them, we grappled crossways; we'd always hook onto 'em.

The former sheriff told the story of an unwitting fisher-woman, a lucky one among those who tangled with road and river in the canyon. The young woman was on the way to Aspen for some skiing. State patrolman Jack Kelly and his wife, in their privately owned vehicle, were following the woman and "saw her swerve out, and off in the river she went. So they immediately stopped and went down to help her get out."

While efforts to extricate the car were underway, the woman reached Aspen, where Sheriff Baker later talked with her. He told her they'd removed her car from the river and saved her skis and some clothing. Baker also surprised her with a question:

'By the way, do you have a fishing license?' And she said, 'What would I need a fishing license for?' And I said, 'Well, there was a fish in your car, and it was in your possession.'

He then put the visitor's mind at ease by explaining that the "big ole sucker in the back seat of the car, just floppin' around" had entered through a window while the car was submerged in the river. Officers had a good laugh over that. As Baker said, "You have to have a certain amount of humor in those things, or you'd go crazy."

Sometimes it was necessary to set up road blocks in the canyon:

That was a fine place to throw up a road block, because they had the river on one side and a mountain on the other side. But most of the time, those road blocks would be put up in assistance to some adjoining county's sheriff who would want us to look for and stop a particular car.

Conrad F. Schader

View to east near Mile Mark 127, September 1972. Reverse Curve Tunnel was bored for I-70 in cliff shown.

As sheriff, Baker had additional responsibilities as the county's fire warden. Fires in the canyon were most often along the railroad tracks and resulted from hotboxes on rail cars.

There were climbers who became trapped on cliff ledges and were unable to climb farther up or go back down, but those occurrences were unusual. Baker said that climbing mishaps seemed to become more common in the 1960s. And drug traffic increased around that time and required more attention from law officers.

Baker retired in January 1975 despite the enthusiasm of constituents who urged him to seek yet another term. In his early 80s and living in Grand Junction, he said in 1993 that he still held the record for longest period of service as sheriff of the county.

When Baker became sheriff, there were only two people in the department — Baker and an undersheriff:

My wife did the cooking for the prisoners, and I was the jailor and the sheriff and the investigator; you name it. We finally wound up with five of us at the sheriffs office when I retired, and they tell me now there's 37.

I was proud of my 22 years as sheriff of Garfield County. I must have done something right, because they kept putting me back in there.

Aerial view of No Name area, west end of Glenwood Canyon,
September 1971. Short stretch of new highway was completed from
No Name west through twin tunnels to Glenwood Springs in 1965.
U.S. 6 & 24 route around horseshoe bend, seen at left, was bypassed.

VII

CANYON LINK COMPLETES I-70

President Dwight D. Eisenhower in the 1950s backed creation of an interstate highway system to improve transportation in peacetime and serve as a vital network for defense in the event of war. Establishment of an interstate system received congressional approval in 1956. Four years later, Eisenhower signed legislation authorizing appropriation of federal funds for a segment of interstate between Denver and Cove Fort, Utah.

More than 30 years passed before a completed interstate stretched across Colorado in an east-west direction. The segment through Glenwood Canyon was the final link, a stretch made possible only with the deployment of innovations in design, construction, project management, and public participation.

OPPOSITION THREATENS PROJECT

When a proposed I-70 route through Glenwood Canyon became known, strong opposition arose and swelled eventually to such a degree that it jeopardized the project. Glenwood Springs citizens saw construction creep through the northeast part of their town and pierce the canyon's west edge with twin tunnels completed in fall 1965. While that construction bypassed a troublesome horseshoe bend in U.S. 6 and 24, citizens decried the traditional cut-and-fill method with its severe alteration of the canyon walls to make room for the highway. And some criticized the design of the twin tunnels as unattractive and unimaginative.

The eruption of opposition that began in the 1960s intensified and persisted through the first half of the 1970s. Protests ranged from fiery letters to newspaper editors to demonstrations within the canyon. There were lawsuits, hearings, additional surveys, and the time-consuming involvement of scores of government agencies.

Environmental groups and other opponents favored preservation or modification of the existing highway. They maintained that an interstate spelled ruination for the canyon environment, including the aesthetic aspects. They claimed that the cost of paving the old highway with silver dollars would be less than the price of an interstate. And they said the existing highway at 40 miles per hour was safer than the proposed 55-mile-per-hour I-70. Some critics argued that a four-lane highway, with the probably necessity of elevating one or more lanes, would make the canyon walls less impressive and decrease perception of the canyon's depth.

On one occasion, entertainer John Denver joined protestors in the canyon to demonstrate opposition to the interstate. He complained that the canyon was so narrow that the river level would rise because of dirt and rock fill if the new highway were built. Press reports in advance of the demonstration indicated that Denver would throw a silver dollar across the river to illustrate the narrowness of the canyon.

But distances can be difficult to estimate in the mountains. Former sheriff Ralph Baker recalled that a county commissioner, attempting to show that the river was not all that narrow, handed Denver a rock and said something like, " 'Mister Denver, let's see

Eastbound on U.S. 6
at bridge north of
Shoshone Dam,
June 1977.

Conrad F. Schader

you throw this across the river.' And he backed off and gave it a sling, and it landed right smack in the middle." According to Baker, Denver then looked around and picked up a rock of his own choosing and let it fly, "and it landed about in the same place," much to the amusement of some of the onlookers.

Said canyon resident Thelma Bair, "They found the narrowest spot in the canyon, and he had to make two or three tries before he could throw a silver dollar, whatever, across that river."

Those in favor of the interstate countered with statistics that showed high accident rates and escalating traffic volume. They emphasized that the canyon was already far from pristine, that it had long since been altered, first by the railroad and later by the old highway projects that had cut into the cliffs and pushed debris into the river to make room for the highway. Proponents included many who worried about running into sightseers slowing to look at the view, stopping to await passage of oncoming traffic before turning left onto one of the approximately two dozen roadside pulloffs, or hugging the center line at a crawl because of fear of the curves. Many drivers became irritated when these impediments resulted in rapid buildups of traffic that trapped them in long processions of slowly moving vehicles for the duration of the trip through the canyon. Said Thelma Bair, "We knew there had to be a change of some kind. There were too many deaths, too many accidents, too many blind curves."

Alternatives Discussed

Some people suggested a four-lane route over Cottonwood Pass as an alternative. They claimed it would be less costly than

This page and next: Glenwood Canyon.

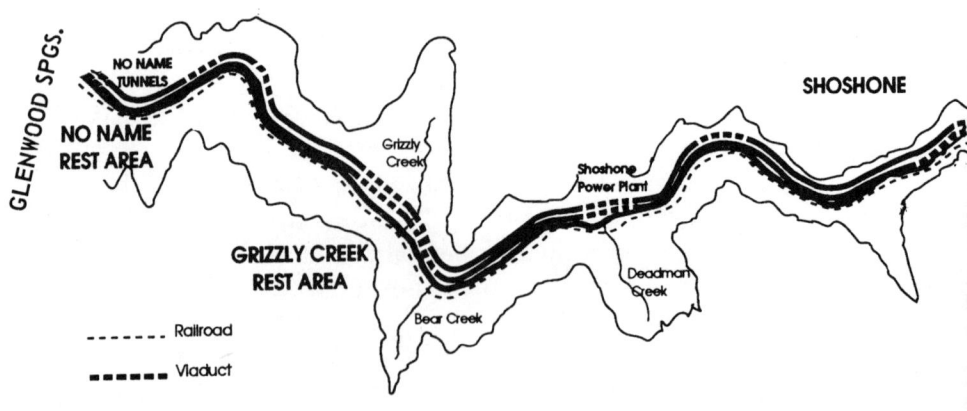

the canyon route. The idea gained considerable support, but it also drew opposition. The Cottonwood alternative stretched 27 miles from Gypsum, climbing across the pass, traveling west, and descending to State Highway 82 in the Roaring Fork Valley.

Said Thelma Bair, "It would have had to come out of Gypsum and gone over Red Hill and Cottonwood Pass. That would never have worked, because it's so high, and the road would have been so bad and so snowy in the wintertime." She said the trucks would have continued to use Glenwood Canyon, because it was shorter and easier.

Planners in fact considered not only Cottonwood Pass south of the canyon but a possible alternative to the north across the Flat Tops. Neither alternative was acceptable in light of technical complications, costs, severe winter weather, environmental concerns, and the distances involved.

A three-lane highway also was considered for the canyon.

Adapted from map released to news media, 1992, by Colorado Department of Transportation.

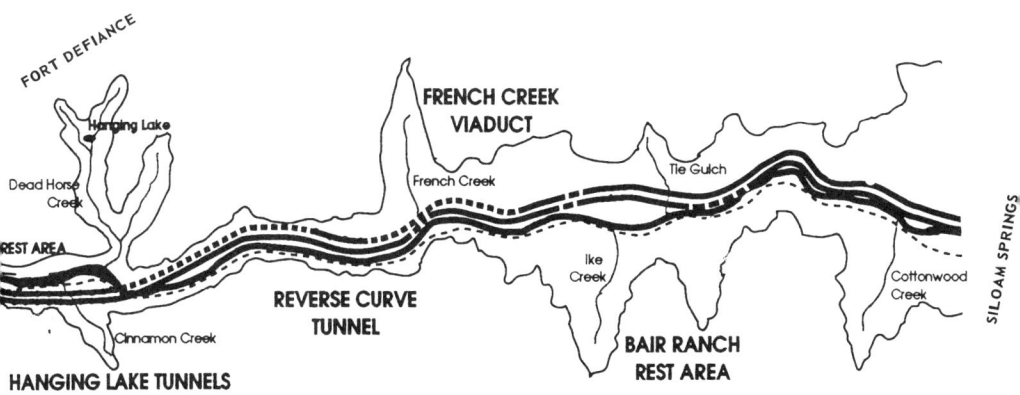

That possibility was rejected, because the minimum width of a three-lane was as much as that of a narrow four-lane. Further, statistics revealed high accident rates on three-lane highways.

DISSENT, COMPLEXITY CHALLENGE DESIGNERS

In 1968, the Colorado General Assembly made a pivotal decision. It passed a resolution in response to growing opposition to the new highway. While the resolution lacked the force of law, it left no doubt that legislators intended the highway to be a tasteful blend between "the wonder of human engineering" and the "wonders of nature."

Designing a highway that would meet transportation needs through the canyon was itself a difficult job. But the necessity to create a transportation corridor that had aesthetic appeal, preserved the environment, and enhanced the canyon's recreational values gave designers a powerful challenge complicated by continued opposition.

Advisory Panels Ease the Way

Colorado Department of Highways assembled a design team headed by the state's project manager Ralph Trapani. Responsibilities of the team included supervision of construction and preparation of plans for mitigation of environmental damage and alteration. Among members of the team were two outstanding designers — Joseph R. Passonneau, serving as project director for the group responsible for design of I-70 in the western half of the canyon, and Edgardo Contini acting in the same capacity for the eastern half.

Opposition to the project led to formation of two additional groups — a technical review panel and a citizens advisory committee. Members of the technical review group represented the interests of government agencies and private organizations. Appointed to the seven-member citizens advisory committee

Above: Westbound view from pulloff about one mile east of
Hanging Lake Trailhead, September 1983.
Below: Eastbound view, Loretta and Frank Schader at
Shoshone Power Plant, October 1976.

Photos by Conrad F. Schader

were four people from areas affected by the construction and one member each from the American Institute of Architects, Colorado Open Space Council, and Club 20 — an organization that represents Western Slope viewpoints.

While the operations of these panels failed to immediately quiet the dissent, they heavily influenced the design and construction of the highway, the rest areas, and the provisions for recreational use of the canyon. The work of these groups averted catastrophic litigation, and perhaps legislation, that might have derailed the canyon project.

In addition, there were community workshops open to interested citizens. About 30 local people took part.

Consideration of a wide range of viewpoints resulted in commitments: The project must preserve the natural environment and enhance recreation values. The highway must blend visually with the canyon. And the canyon must remain open to traffic during the construction years.

Passonneau Reveals Design Process

In a 1981 technical paper, designer Joseph R. Passonneau described the study and display methods used in the preliminary design work. Among resources employed were ordinary sketches, photographs, drawings of terrain cross sections from a viewpoint 25 feet above U.S. Highway 6 and 24, environmental strip maps, computer-drawn cross sections, composites made by drawing alternative designs on photos, full-scale and small-scale models, cartoons presenting complex concepts in simple terms, and isometric drawings.*

Passonneau pointed out that all of these resources are means of communication, and that communication in all of its forms is the well-spring of a designer's creative process. For instance, sketches showed the canyon to be a series of "outdoor rooms

---

* Passonneau defined an isometric projection as a "perspective projection from a particular point of view."

Bill Echols photo   DMJM Architects & Engineers

Citizens Advisory Committee examines 1989 progress on I-70 in
canyon. At front of group is designer Joseph R. Passonneau.

with transitions that could be dramatized by highway design."
The character of the east half of the canyon was different from
that of the west half. The east half was U-shaped, while the
west was V-shaped. The varying kinds of rock and rock formations, plant communities, the river and its tributaries, trails,
buildings, and scars from old construction all required consideration in the design.

Four-lane I-70 not only had to fit into the rugged canyon but
had to do so on the same path as the existing highway. In addition, the proposed designs faced reviewers from diverse back-
grounds and representing a variety of interests including more
than 60 government agencies, environmental and recreational

Westbound at
Mile Mark 126
west of
French Creek,
October 1976.

Conrad F. Schader

organizations, and the technical review and citizens advisory groups. As a result, the project required preparation of an unusually large number of design alternatives.

Colorado Approves Project, Adopts Citizen Recommendations

The Colorado Highway Commission in 1977 approved construction of four-lane Interstate 70 through Glenwood Canyon. Late that year, the state awarded a contract to L and M Enterprises of Berthoud, Colorado, for landscape tests. The contract covered a sprinkler system and the planting of various grasses and shrubs on test plots at No Name and French Creek so that planners could study survival and maturity rates and decide which varieties were most appropriate for I-70 landscaping.

Highway officials scheduled a public hearing for March 1978 in Glenwood Springs concerning recommended design of I-70 in the canyon. In advance of the hearing, realistic models and other exhibits detailing the design and the alternative concepts considered during the two-year design process went on public display at Hotel Colorado.

Some 300 people attended the formal hearing, and *The Denver Post* reported public reaction to the design was "generally favorable." About 50 people testified. Executive Director Jack Kinstlinger of the Colorado Department of Highways, in a letter published by the *Rocky Mountain News*, said the testimony

Part of lifelike model illustrating a design for I-70 in Grizzly Creek area. Model was one of exhibits at Hotel Colorado in advance of March 1978 public hearing. Exhibits prepared by DeLeuw, Cather & Company; DMJM Phillips-Reister; Gruen Associates.

Conrad F. Schader

Conrad F. Schader

At Mile Mark 126, looking east toward Reverse Curve,
September 1979.

was " 'predominantly in favor of the design as proposed by the department.' " Nevertheless, some voices rose in dissent, and some vowed continuation of efforts to block construction.

D. Blake Chambliss, a member of the citizens advisory committee, said the panel "agonized over each specific recommendation." In a 1978 article in *The Denver Post*, Chambliss wrote that completion of a widely acceptable design was possible because the committee took into consideration "all possible voices during the design process."

Final recommendations by the committee included a number of variations from interstate standards, variations granted by federal legislation. As a case in point, the final design of the four-lane highway called for an overall width of 68 feet instead of the standard 104 feet.

The final design incorporated some other recommendations by the committee. Recognizing " 'the immense recreational value of Hanging Lake,' " the panel called for the highway to cross the river and railroad on viaducts just east of Cinnamon Creek, pass through twin 3,900-foot tunnels, and return down river to the north bank. This was the only place in the canyon where I-70 left the old U.S. 6 and 24 path along the north bank. This special routing made space for a rest area and returned a mile-long " 'scenic room' " in the Hanging Lake area to its most natural state, free of traffic sights and sounds.

The design included a control center for tunnel operations and a temporary bridge downstream from the Hanging Lake Trailhead for construction access to the site of the tunnels from the old highway on the river's north side. It adopted recommendations for terraced, independent alignment of the westbound and eastbound lanes and included a recreation path beside the river.

PURSUING CONSTRUCTION DETAILS, HAPPENINGS

Quoted in a *Rocky Mountain News* article, Mike Herron of the Federal Highway Administration in Denver said the project was " 'huge, complicated' " and a " 'unique situation in this country, and perhaps . . . the world.' " Engineers expended 800,000 hours developing the construction techniques that made the highway possible.

Construction Begins

Nielsons, Inc. of Cortez, Colorado started work on improvement of the No Name Interchange in April 1980. More contractors moved people and equipment into the canyon in

September 1981 and initiated new construction. Peter Kiewit and Sons Construction Company began work on the highway itself — a mile-long segment near No Name.

As the massive undertaking gained momentum, hundreds of additional workers settled into the area, many of them moving into mobile home parks such as the Malpals settlement at Dotsero. The daily work force eventually reached 500. And designers and builders from many countries came to study the landmark project.

In 1982, the first of three fatal accidents occurred on the canyon project. On the morning of July 2, a one-ton weight fell from a crane and struck 49-year-old construction worker Frank Berg on the head. The accident near Dotsero also involved a metal hook that struck the Oregon man on the leg. Berg died about two hours later at Valley View Hospital in Glenwood Springs.

River Adds to Difficulties

Forecasts of high water in 1984 prompted maintenance workers to enlarge a small berm constructed the previous year between Bair Ranch and French Creek to protect U.S. 6 and 24. Rising above its levels of the previous year, the river became engorged with a flow of 23,000 cubic feet per second. It reached a level as much as four feet above the highway, breached the enlarged berm at the start of Memorial Day weekend, and sloshed across the highway. Except for a closure lasting several hours, highway crews working 18-hour shifts through the weekend, and aided by contractors working in the canyon, were able to keep the highway open.

Meantime, the Rio Grande fought its own battle. The swollen river flooded the tracks and eroded the railbed. Rio Grande suspended freight traffic, and Amtrak re-routed its California Zephyr through Wyoming, while Rio Grande labored to stabilize the south bank of the river with fill material brought into the canyon on a work train from Dotsero.

Conrad F. Schader

Eastbound about one mile east of No Name during construction of
upper (westbound) lanes of I-70, August 1985.

Loretta B. Schader

Westbound on nearly completed lower lanes of I-70, August 1985.
Both westbound and eastbound traffic used lower lanes
during construction of upper (westbound) lanes
seen in progress at right.

The year 1984 brought snowslide problems as well. Around March, slides buried sections of track with snow, trees, and rocks. Serious delays resulted.

Restraining Order Sought

With construction of some portions already completed, a coalition of opponents, including the Colorado Open Space Council and the Sierra Club, went to court in Denver in 1984. They attempted to convince a federal judge to issue a restraining order blocking construction through a particularly narrow part of the canyon. U.S. District Judge John Kane rejected the coalition's request in June, citing a lack of evidence that the construction threatened irreparable damage to the canyon.

Consultant Engineers Gridlock Solution

When construction gained momentum and more and more contractors moved into the canyon, traffic problems developed. *The Denver Post* cited figures from Department of Highways district engineer Dick Prosence indicating a marked increase in traffic through the canyon. Highest daily volume in 1978 was 10,000 vehicles. On a peak day in summer 1981, the count exceeded 13,000. The increase in traffic volume was not in itself responsible for the jams that developed. Rather, the increase exacerbated an underlying problem.

Conforming with standard practice, contractors exercised individual control of traffic through their respective work areas. But so many contractors in the canyon's limited space, and no practical detours, soon made the use of traditional methods of traffic control unacceptable.

Traffic released by one contractor faced additional stops when it entered construction zones controlled by other contractors. Traffic jams formed, and vehicles backed up not only at a given contractor's holding point but into the work areas of other contractors nearby. By late 1984, gridlock became so

Bill Echols photo   DMJM Architects and Engineers

I-70 construction, spring 1991, seen from west portals
of Hanging Lake Tunnels.

severe that travelers sometimes spent two hours negotiating the 12.5-mile canyon. Tensions developed between travelers and contractors and among contractors themselves. The need for a new approach to traffic control was obvious and urgent.

Colorado Department of Highways turned to Daniel, Mann, Johnson, and Mendenhall (DMJM) — the department's management consultant on the project — for a solution. DMJM designed, implemented, and operated a unique program of traffic control that attracted worldwide attention.

In essence, the program called for cooperation among contractors, traffic control centralized under a single authority, a communications network including two-way radios, a coordinator to direct all traffic movements, and pilot cars to guide bunches of vehicles alternately westbound and eastbound on a single lane of road through the series of construction zones without stopping at every zone.

According to Hermann A. Guenther, DMJM project manager during part of the construction period, the system went into full operation in the mid 1980s and succeeded beyond expectations, generally limiting delays during peak times to a single stop lasting an average of 30 minutes, expediting passage of emergency vehicles, markedly decreasing the accident rate, and allowing more efficient movement of construction equipment. Under this innovative program, the flaggers directed movement of construction equipment rather than vehicles of the motoring public. Meantime, personnel at the traffic stops contacted drivers in the waiting lines, informed them of the expected length of delay, and answered questions about the canyon work.

The traffic program received the Transportation Achievement Award for Operations in 1986 from the Institute of Transportation Engineers.

Flaggers See Much Good, Some Bad

Flaggers reported that most motorists were courteous. "Most were angels," said one woman in a radio interview. But

Fred R. Allen photo   Fred R. Allen collection

Erection gantry in action, October 1991.

there were a few who threw insults and various objects, such as beer cans and even dirty diapers, at flaggers. Turnover on that job was high, mainly because of weather extremes and monotony. Flaggers received $9.50 per hour plus benefits.

Trainmen often honked the horns of their locomotives at flaggers. Said retired engineer Louis Petrafeso, "We used to honk, and they'd wave at us. We got to the point that, when we figured they were flag girls, we'd throw 'em a kiss. I did that until one day I threw one at a long-haired boy. That was the end of that."

Engineers Take Highway from Design to Reality

At the suggestion of the citizens advisory panel, the highway used terraced retaining walls and a pavement base of concrete slabs that cantilevered six feet beyond the faces of the walls. According to an article by DMJM project manager Hermann Guenther, the position of the lower (eastbound) road with respect to the upper (westbound) road, and the heights of the retaining walls, were "dictated by the steepness of slopes above and below the old highway." Retaining walls were nearly 40 feet high in places.

Construction of the lower lanes took place first. The first task in the sequence was the placement of a concrete footing. Next came fastening of prefabricated retaining walls to the footing. After backfilling, the sequence involved positioning and post-tensioning of the nine-inch-thick concrete slabs, fitting of the parapet and guard rail, and paving with asphalt. The completed eastbound lanes then provided a channel for traffic while construction efforts focused on the westbound lanes.

Some construction methods used in the canyon were new to the United States. The project included nearly 40 bridges and viaducts, most of them intended not for stream crossings but to lessen the highway's impact on the environment. To minimize environmental damage by the construction process itself, special equipment was necessary.

The use of an erection gantry imported from Europe avoided problems where conventional equipment posed a threat to the environment. Employing the " 'balanced cantilever method,' " the gantry made possible the construction of bridges from above after piers and abutments were in place.

The gantry was a 350-foot-long, rigid framework (truss) standing on eight legs. According to DMJM project manager Hermann Guenther in a *TR News* article, precast bridge segments were transported along the gantry and fastened to previously installed segments on alternating sides of a pier. When the trailing segments from the pier neared the segments attached to the previous pier, "a closure segment" was "poured in place," and the gantry was moved to the next pier. Canyon structures erected with the aid of the gantry included the French Creek and Hanging Lake viaducts.

During later years of construction, a contractor established farm plots within the canyon for propagation of plants and production of seeds. This made possible the use of native plants for revegetation of areas disturbed during construction. Extensive networks of tubing drip watered the plants for a couple of years at their final locations. After that, those that survived were on their own. Revegetation included the placement of more than 150,000 individual shrubs and trees.

Blasting was kept to a minimum. Where it was necessary, the newly exposed rock was stained to match the appearance of naturally weathered surfaces. Environmental limits were established. If crews and equipment ventured beyond the limits, they were subject to fines. In some cases, even individual trees within construction areas were designated as untouchable. And Colorado Department of Transportation said in a news release that adjustment of the highway alignment "by inches in order to satisfy geometric, environmental, and aesthetic constraints was not uncommon." As a pilot project to reduce Colorado's mountainous accumulations of discarded tires, contractors made use of shredded tires in backfill and embankment work.

Beside U.S. 6 and 24 were many places for motorists to pull off the highway. Some of them had picnic tables and trash barrels. I-70 eliminated these pulloffs and replaced them with four rest areas providing parking, restrooms, picnic spots, drinking water, and access to the recreation path and river. Cantilevering the ten-foot-wide recreation path from retaining walls avoided encroachment on the river in areas of severely limited space.

The driver of a dump truck in 1985 became the second person to die in construction-related accidents on the canyon project. The *Glenwood Post* reported that the truck driven by 52-year-old Frank Eugene Arbaney of Silt, Colorado, left Highway

6 in the predawn hours of July 30. The truck rolled onto its left side, with the cab landing in shallow water in the river about a mile east of the Hanging Lake parking area. Firefighters freed the unconscious Arbaney from the truck, and he arrived at the Glenwood Springs hospital about three hours after the accident. He died of head injuries shortly after arrival.

Viaduct Complements Canyon

The French Creek Viaduct, consisting of two bridges and a 330-foot at-grade section, carries westbound traffic from the Bair Ranch area to the Reverse Curve Tunnel.* The long, graceful sweep of the viaduct is a good example of a complementary blend of highway and canyon.

When work began with the erection gantry at the viaduct in September 1988, the gantry lost its balance, causing hours of anxiety and a precautionary closure of U.S. 6 and 24. According to a source close to the scene and a *Glenwood Post* article, the problem arose at the first expansion joint just east of French Creek. When crews attempted a launch from pier to pier, failure of an unfinished concrete bridge support placed the entire weight of the gantry on the expansion joint, the joint broke, and the truss tilted and swayed downward about four feet, came back up a couple of feet, and stopped. There were fears of danger to traffic in the event the gantry slipped farther. Officials closed the highway for several hours while the contractor and state personnel devised a plan and stabilized the gantry.

They counterweighted the gantry with rolls of tendon material, the half-inch rod used for strengthening of concrete, and about 20 sections of concrete road barrier, a total weight of 100,000 pounds. Then they "walked" the gantry back and restarted the launch process.

---

* Reverse Curve Tunnel received its name from a river bend that changes direction, similar to an *S curve*.

Two views of gantry with a segment of French Creek Viaduct, 1988.

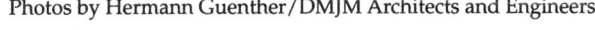

Photos by Hermann Guenther/DMJM Architects and Engineers

Tunnel Complex Exemplifies Technology

The Hanging Lake Tunnel complex immediately west of Cinnamon Creek is the result of innovative design, employment of latest construction techniques, and use of technologically advanced equipment. The complex consists of twin tunnels in quartzite rock and an operations and control center.

Colorado Department of Transportation said in a news release that the complex was "considered to be the most sophisticated tunnel operation in the U.S." Contractor for the project was a joint venture comprised of two firms headquartered in Evansville, Indiana, and one each from Austria and West Germany. From the design by Parsons Brinkerhoff, the venture company produced an engineering marvel.

Rock reinforcements — rock bolts and shotcrete (epoxy) — made the bores self supporting, the first use of this system in the United States. This technique made the traditional steel and concrete arches unnecessary. Thus, the interior finish existed for cosmetic purposes, and probably for improved lighting and airflow efficiency, rather than for structural integrity. A concrete lining served as a suitable base for the overlying ceramic tiles.

The control center, itself a technological masterwork, occupies a four-story structure nearly buried in the slope above the tunnels. The building contains sophisticated control and monitoring equipment, offices, and the ventilation system for the tunnels.

Nearly 20 video cameras as well as sensors for temperature, moisture, ice, and carbon monoxide, feed a continuous flow of information about the tunnels and their environment to controlroom technicians. With the aid of this advanced equipment, operators are aware of each individual vehicle and know whether it exits or remains inside.

The ventilation system for the tunnels is reversable. Its 300-horsepower fans can exhaust polluted air from the bores or force in fresh air. Emergency equipment and vehicles stand in readiness within the complex.

Fred R. Allen photo   Fred R. Allen collection

I-70 construction, west portals of Hanging Lake Tunnels,
October 1991.

A rebroadcast system allows motorists to pass through the
tunnels with no loss of radio reception. This system is also use-
ful in an emergency, because it allows tunnel personnel to inter-
rupt the rebroadcasts and transmit safety bulletins.

Conrad F. Schader

Part of Hanging Lake Tunnels controlroom, October 13, 1992.

Two Emergencies, Return of Bighorns Noted

On the canyon wall about eight miles east of Glenwood Springs and three hundred feet above the highway, loomed an overhanging mass of rock about the size of a house. Engineers believed the rock, called the Bee Hive, might eventually break loose. Removal of this hazard closed the canyon for more than eight hours on October 16, 1990 and resulted in an exciting detour for a woman on the way to the hospital in Glenwood Springs. Two blasts dislodged the threatening rock, and the debris choked a 200-foot section of highway in the Hanging Lake area. Meantime, a Gypsum woman went into premature labor, and an ambulance drove her to the east end of the rock debris. Foreseeing such an emergency, planners had a motor-boat in the river near the blast area. The boat carried the

Conrad F. Schader

Part of Grizzly Creek Rest Area, October 13, 1992. Building contains restrooms. Special septic system converts waste to fertilizer.

woman safely downstream to a waiting ambulance at the west end of the highway blockage.

A 65-year-old Rifle, Colorado crane operator died in 1991 of injuries received in a fall near Reverse Curve. The *Glenwood Post* said that Joseph Kuberry reportedly slipped on ice on the morning of March 12 and fell into a 12-foot-deep hole while helping to clear snow from a construction area beside the recreation path. The hole had been dug in connection with installation of a box culvert intended to carry the path beneath the highway. Kuberry died soon after arrival at Valley View Hospital.

In order to avoid accidents and the disruptive effects of construction on the canyon's Rocky Mountain Bighorn Sheep, Colorado trapped the animals and removed them from the canyon in the early 1970s. The I-70 design included passageways intended to give animals safe access to the river. After completion of segments incorporating these small tunnels beneath the highway, Colorado Division of Wildlife reintroduced the sheep. Wildlife personnel released 27 Bighorns near the canyon's west end in 1990 and 20 more in 1991 near Grizzly Creek.

HIGHWAY DEBUT DRAWS RAVE REVIEWS

Despite the project's complexity and immensity, and delays caused by protests, legal challenges, and regulatory hurdles, completion of the canyon highway came one year ahead of schedule. While a number of details, such as finishing work on rest areas and some final paving, extended the 490-million-dollar project into the next year, Colorado Department of Transportation opened the canyon highway on the morning of October 14, 1992.* More than 1,000 people crowded into the eastbound bore of the Hanging Lake Tunnels for opening ceremonies, during which Governor Roy Romer snipped the ribbon to officially open this final link in I-70 through Colorado. If there were still some negative voices deriding the highway, they were unheard amidst a veritable chorus of praise and approval for the interstate, its designers, and its builders.

Designer Edgardo Contini did not live to see completion of the Glenwood highway. But Joseph R. Passonneau, Contini's counterpart for the western half, witnessed the full translation of the inspired designs by both men into four lanes of steel, concrete, and asphalt that not only served their transportation purpose but met the ancient canyon in artistic and complementary ways. The canyon project received the national Outstanding Civil Engineering Achievement award for 1993 from the American Society of Civil Engineers.

The interstate is undisputably a milestone in environmentally sensitive construction, a state-of-the-art marriage between canyon and highway, and a tribute to the people who participated in the

---

* Colorado Highway Department had become the Colorado Department of Transportation in 1991.

Photos by Conrad F. Schader

Above: Inside eastbound Hanging Lake Tunnel, October 13, 1992 —
day before dedication.
Below: View to the east from westbound lanes of I-70 at French Creek,
October 13, 1992.

I-70 IN GLENWOOD CANYON, SOME FACTS
(Most figures are approximations)

Project Cost: $490,348,000
Funding: 90% federal, 10% state
Construction Duration: 12 years
Total Number of Workers: 1,000
Maximum Daily Workforce: 500
Construction-Related Accidental Deaths: 3
Construction Contracts: 35-40
Bridges & Viaducts: 39, total length 6.5 miles
Retaining Walls: 20 miles combined length
Concrete Used: 1.62 billion pounds
Reinforcing Steel: 30,000,000 pounds
Structural Steel: 30,000,000 pounds
Landscaping and Revegetation: 150,000 trees and shrubs

French Creek Viaduct Length: 4,000 feet
    (two bridges & 330-foot section at grade)

Hanging Lake Tunnels
    Length, each bore: 3,900 feet
    Construction explosives used: $1,000,000 worth
    Rock removed: 250,000 cubic yards
    East end viaducts, number of concrete segments: 1,200

Some Key Participants
    Project Manager for Colorado: Ralph Trapani
    Supervising Architect: DeLeuw, Cather and Company
    Designers: Edgardo Contini (east half), Joseph R. Passonneau
        (west half)
    Management Consultant: Daniel, Mann, Johnson and Mendenhall

Special Panels
    Design team comprised of subgroups for east and west halves
    Technical Review Group
    Citizens Advisory Committee

Principal Source: Colorado Department of Transportation
Chart by Conrad F. Schader

design and construction. While it has a different look for the fourth time since work began on the Taylor State Road nearly one hundred years ago, the canyon remains one of Colorado's great, natural attractions. Travelers continue to exclaim over it, take its picture, and carry it home among their memories.

In the early 1990s, telecommunications companies laid fiberoptic cable beneath the railroad. And so, this scenic canyon, already a corridor for a river, railroad, interstate highway, and recreation path, became a conduit for yet another transportation system — the information highway.

GLENWOOD CANYON TRAILS

TRAIL	TRAILHEAD LOCATION	MILES ONE WAY	REMARKS
Canyon Recreation	Both ends of canyon	16.5	Paved. East end parking reached via Dotsero, Exit 132. West parking at Glenwood Springs. Path intersects canyon's rest areas and side trails.
French Creek	Recreation path	0.33	Old road that follows creek along jungle-like side canyon.
Hanging Lake	About 0.5 mile east of Hanging Lake Rest Area on recreation path	1.0	Hanging Lake Rest Area not accessible from westbound I-70.
Grizzly Creek	Grizzly Creek Rest Area	3.5	First 0.25 mile suitable for wheelchairs. Hikers can ascend to point where vegetation & narrowing of side canyon create impassable jungle. Upper part joined by connecting link to No Name Trail.
No Name	Just north of No Name Rest Area	5.75	Begins as road about 0.25 mile north of No Name Interchange and leads to the Flat Tops. Upper part meets connecting link running eastward to Grizzly Creek Trail.

Sources: various
Chart by Conrad F. Schader

BIBLIOGRAPHY

Allen, Fred R., Grand Junction, Colo. Personal Communication, February 22, 1994.

Allen, Norma, Grand Junction, Colo. Personal Communication, February 9, 1994.

Avalanche (Glenwood Springs), Selected dates.

Bair, Elmer O. *Elmer Bair's Story*. Carbondale, Colo.: Gran Farnum Printing and Publishing, 1987.

———., of Carbondale, Colo. Personal Communications, November 19, 1993, January 13, 1994.

Bair, J. Golden, Glenwood Canyon. Personal Communication, November 8, 1993.

Bair, Thelma, Glenwood Canyon. Personal Communication, November 8, 1993.

Baker, James H., and LeRoy R. Hafen, editors. *History of Colorado*, Vol. I. Denver: Linderman, 1927.

Baker, Ralph, Grand Junction, Colo. Personal Communication, October 8, 1993.

Bauer, William H., and others. *Colorado Postal History*. Crete, Neb.: J-B Publishing, 1971.

Bowhay, Ruth (Mrs. Cecil Bowhay), Grand Junction, Colo. Personal Communication, August 7, 1993.

Brown, Dr. Woodrow E., Hotchkiss, Colo. Personal Communication, April 5, 1995.

Burlington, Rio Grande, Western Pacific. *Vista-Dome Views*. Brochure promoting California Zephyr, February 15, 1956.

Cahill, Rick. *Colorado Hot Springs Guide*. Boulder, Colo.: Pruett, 1986.

Campbell, John A., and others. *Paleozoic Stratigraphy and Structural Evolution of Colorado*. Richard H. De Voto, editor, Published as *Quarterly of the Colorado School of Mines*, Vol. 67, No. 4 (October 1972).

Chronic, Halka. *Roadside Geology of Colorado*. Missoula, Mont.: Mountain Press, 1980.

Chronic, John, and Halka Chronic. *Prairie Peak and Plateau*, Colo. Geological Survey Bulletin 32. Denver: Colorado Geological Survey, 1972.

Colorado Historical Society. *Colorado Magazine*, various issues.

Colorado Secretary of State records, Denver.

Colorado Writers' Project, Work Projects Administration. *Colorado*. New York: Hastings House, 1941.

Crofutt, George A. *Crofutt's Grip-Sack Guide of Colorado*, 1885. Omaha: Overland Publishing.

Dawson, J. Frank. *Place Names in Colorado*. Denver: J. Frank Dawson Publishing, 1954.

Dennison, William D., Denver. Personal Communications, May 7, 1993, March 25, 1995.

The Denver Post, Numerous issues, 1965-1982, selected earlier and later dates.

Eberhart, Perry. *The Guide To The Colorado Ghost Towns and Mining Camps*. Denver: Sage Books, 1959.

Echols, Bill, Denver. Personal Communications, August 4, 30, 1993.

Ellis, Erl H. *Colorado Mapology*. Frederick, Colo.: Jende-Hagan Book Corp., 1983.

Erickson, Kenneth A., and Albert W. Smith. *Atlas of Colorado*. Boulder: Colorado Associated University Press, 1985.

Forney, Gerald G., Denver. Personal Communications, September 22, 1993, March 2, 1994.

Frost, Kenny, Glenwood Springs. Personal Communication, April 28, 1995.

Glenwood Post (Glenwood Springs), Selected dates.

Green, Abel, and Joe Laurie, Jr. *Show Biz*. New York: Henry Holt, 1951.

Griswold, Don, and others. *Colorado's Century of "Cities."* Denver: Smith-Brooks Printing, 1958.

Guenther, Hermann. "A Coordinated Approach To Traffic Control Management Through Multiple Highway Construction Contracts." A paper presented at Joint International Conference, Transportation Research Board & Swedish Road and Traffic Research Institute, Gothenburg, September 28, 1989.

——. "Blending the Wonders of Engineering and Nature." *TR News*, No. 153 (March-April 1991).

——. Denver, Personal Communication, July 13, 1993.

Haberman, Pauline C., and others. *I-70 Glenwood Canyon*. Denver: Colorado Department of Transportation, U.S. Department of Transportation, 1992.

Hafen, LeRoy R., and Ann Hafen. *The Colorado Story*. Denver: Old West, 1953.

Hall, Frank. *History of the State of Colorado*, 4 vols. Chicago: Blakely Printing, 1889-1895.

Harland, W. Brian, and others. *A geologic time scale 1989*. New York: University of Cambridge Press Syndicate, 1990.

Hart, Don. *Tim Kelley's Colorado Fishing, Hunting & Outdoor Guide*. Denver: Don Hart, 1990.

Hayden, F. V., and others. *Geological and Geographical Atlas of Colorado*. Washington, D.C.: U.S. Department of Interior, 1877.

Hotel Committee. *Colorado Towns and Resorts*. Denver: Freemasons, 1892.

Hudson, Darrell, Wheat Ridge, Colo. Personal Communication, April 8, 1995.

Hughes, J. Donald. *American Indians in Colorado*. Boulder, Colo.: Pruett, 1987.

Hunt, Charles. B. "Geologic History of the Colorado River," in *The Colorado River Region and John Wesley Powell*, U.S. Geological Survey Prof. Paper 669. Washington, D.C.: U.S. Government Printing Office, 1969.

Jefferson, James, and others. *The Southern Utes*. Ignacio, Colo.: Southern Ute Tribe, 1972.

Jocknick, Sidney. *Early Days on the Western Slope of Colorado*. Denver: Carson-Harper, 1913.

Kernochan, Abby L. "Postal Lists of Colorado, 1859 to Dec. 1, 1881." Typescript. n.p., 1969 [?].

Kight, Bill, Glenwood Springs. Personal Communication, April 28, 1995.

Knupp. Laurene Grant, Eagle, Colo. Personal Communication, April 2, 1996.

Koonce, Alice M., Eagle, Colo. Personal Communication, April 2, 1996.

Lathrop, Gilbert A. *Little Engines and Big Men*. Caldwell, Idaho: Caxton Printers, 1955.

———. *Rio Grande Glory Days*. San Marino, Calif.: Golden West Books, 1976.

Lavender, David. *The Big Divide*. Garden City, N.Y.: Doubleday, 1949.

Marsh, Charles S. *People of the Shining Mountains*. Boulder, Colo.: Pruett, 1982.

McCarthy, G. Michael. *Hour of Trial*. Norman: University of Oklahoma Press, 1977.

McConnell, Virginia. *Bayou Salado*. Denver: Sage Books, 1966.

McGregor, Heather. *A Guide To Glenwood Canyon*. Glenwood Springs: Pika Publishing, 1992.

McTighe, James. *Roadside History of Colorado*. Boulder, Colo.: Johnson, 1989.

Miscellaneous Files. Pamphlets, brochures, & news releases in possession of author.

Miscellaneous Newspapers. Clippings, some sources unidentified, in scrapbooks acquired by Frontier Historical Museum, Glenwood Springs.

Morgan, Lewis H. *Houses and House-Life of the American Aborigines*. Chicago: University of Chicago, 1965. Originally: *Contributions to North American Ethnology*, Vol. IV. Washington, D.C.: U.S. Government Printing Office, 1881.

Nimon, James E., Eagle, Colo. Personal Communication, November 2, 1993.

Ormes, Robert M., editor. *Guide to the Colorado Mountains*. Denver: Sage Books, 1955.

Passonneau, Joseph R. "Isometric Projections and Other Study and Display Methods Used in Preliminary Design of I-70 Through Glenwood Canyon." *Transportation Research Record 806*. Washington, D.C.: National Academy of Sciences, 1981.

Petrafeso, Louis, Grand Junction, Colo. Personal Communication, October 21, 1993.

Pettit, Jan. *The Utes*. Colorado Springs: Century One Press, 1982.

Pihl, Roger. Tour of canyon project for news media. Glenwood Canyon, October 13, 1992.

Powell, J. W. *Canyons of The Colorado*. New York: Argosy-Antiquarian, 1964.

Promotion and Publicity Committee. *Colorado, its Hotels and Resorts*. Denver: 1904.

PSCO Times (Public Service Company of Colorado), Vol. 6, No. 16 (Nov. 14, 1994).

Ray, Louis L. *The Great Ice Age.* U.S. Geological Survey pamphlet. Washington, D.C.: U.S. Government Printing Office, 1992.

Rio Grande Industries, Inc. *Annual Report 1983.*

Rockwell, Wilson. *The Utes.* Denver: Sage Books, 1956.

Rocky Mountain News (Denver), Numerous dates, 1965-1995, selected earlier dates.

Ruffner, Lt. E. H. *Reconnaissance in the Ute Country.* Washington, D.C.: U.S. Government Printing Office, 1874.

Schader, Conrad F. *Colorado's Alluring Tin Cup.* Golden, Colo.: Regio Alta Publications, 1992.

Schoening, John, Grand Junction, Colo. Personal Communication, November 16, 1993.

Schrock, Elwyn, No Name, Colo. Personal Communication, October 27, 1993.

Shikes, Dr. Robert H. *Rocky Mountain Medicine.* Boulder, Colo.: Johnson, 1986.

Shoemaker, Len. *Pioneers of the Roaring Fork.* Denver: Sage Books, 1965.

———. *Roaring Fork Valley.* Denver: Sage Books, 1958.

———. *Saga of a Forest Ranger.* Boulder: University of Colorado Press, 1958.

"Shoshone Hydroelectric Plant." News release, Public Service Company of Colorado and Colorado Department of Transportation, 1992.

Smith, Duane A., and Duane Vandenbusche. *A Land Alone.* Boulder, Colo.: Pruett, 1981.

Stegner, Wallace Earle. *Beyond The Hundredth Meridian.* Boston: Houghton, Mifflin, 1962.

Stokes, William L., and David J. Varnes. *Glossary of Selected Geologic Terms,* Colo. Scientific Soc. Proceedings, Vol. 16. Denver: Colo. Scientific Soc., 1955.

Stone, Wilbur Fisk, editor. *History of Colorado.* Vols. I., III. Chicago: S. J. Clarke Company, 1918.

Urquhart, Lena M. *Cold Snows of Carbonate.* Denver: Golden Bell Press, 1967.

———. *Colorow.* Denver: Golden Bell Press, 1968.

———. *Glenwood Springs.* Boulder, Colo.: Pruett, 1970.

U.S. Forest Service map. "White River National Forest." Washington, D.C.: U.S. Government Printing Office, 1976.

U.S. Geological Survey topographic maps. "Broken Rib Creek," "Carbonate," "Cottonwood Pass," "Dotsero," "Glenwood Springs," "Shoshone" quadrangles, 1987 revisions.

U.S. Land Office records. Bureau of Land Management, Lakewood, Colo.; U.S. Archives and Records Administration, Washington.

U.S. Post Office. "Records of Appointment, Postmasters 1832-Sept. 30, 1971, Garfield County." U.S. Archives and Records Admin., Lakewood, Colo.

Vanderwilt, John W., supervisor. *Mineral Resources of Colorado*. Denver: Colo. Mineral Resources Board, 1947.

Waters, Salma A., editor. *Colorado 1959-1961 Year Book*. Denver: State Planning Commission.

Wheat, Doug. *The Floater's Guide to Colorado*. Billings and Helena, Mont.: Falcon Press Publishing, 1983.

Wilson, O. Meredith. *The Denver and Rio Grande Project, 1870-1901*. Salt Lake City: Howe Bros., 1982.

Wolle, Muriel Sibell. *Stampede to Timberline*, sec. ed., rev. Chicago: Sage Books, 1974.

INDEX

Frank C. Schader photo

The author at Western State College of Colorado library, Gunnison.

ABOUT THE AUTHOR

Conrad Frank Schader has lived in Colorado since 1947 and has worked with the spoken and written word since 1948. In a 38-year radio career spanning responsibilities both on and off the air, Conrad (Con) has held such positions as program director, news director, music director, and sports director.

While his career began with a two-year stay at a Trinidad, Colorado station, he spent the ensuing years in a variety of positions with Denver area stations and delivered many highly rated programs. His assignments included announcing, program hosting, music selecting, audio engineering, and the gathering, writing, editing, and delivering of radio news. Conrad reported on every general election from 1954 through 1984, mostly at the local anchor position. A regional network carried some of his reports. For 1985, he won a Best Sportscast award from the Associated Press.

Con attended Denver University for a time and later received a degree from Metropolitan State College of Denver. His interests ranged from economics to data processing but centered on the past, present, and future of Colorado. Among his hobbies were fishing, hiking, prospecting, and the photographing of subjects in the United States and overseas.

Schader is the author of *Colorado's Alluring Tin Cup*, published by Regio Alta in 1992.